Charitable
Status

A Practical Handbook
6th Edition

Julian Blake

Contributors: Christine Rigby, Alice Faure Walker, Bill Lewis and Rosamund McCarthy

Original author: Andrew Phillips (Lord Phillips of Sudbury OBE)

DIRECTORY OF SOCIAL CHANGE

Published by
The Directory of Social Change
24 Stephenson Way
London NWI 2DP
Tel: 08450 77 77 07, fax: 020 7391 4804
email: info@dsc.org.uk
web: www.dsc.org.uk
from whom further copies and a full publications list are available.

The Directory of Social Change is a Registered Charity no. 800517

First published 1980 by InterChange Books
Second edition 1982
Third edition 1988
Fourth edition 1994 published by Directory of Social Change
Fifth edition 2003
Sixth edition 2008

ISBN 978 1 903991 86 2

British Library Cataloguing in Publication Data
A catalogue record for this book is available from the British Library

Text and cover designed by Sarah Nicholson
Typeset by Marlinzo Services, Somerset
Printed and bound by Page Bros, Norwich

Other Directory of Social Change departments
Training and conferences tel: 08450 77 77 07
Charityfair/Charity Centre tel: 08450 77 77 07
Publicity tel: 08450 77 77 07

Directory of Social Change Northern Office:
Federation House, Hope Street, Liverpool LI 9
Courses and conferences tel: 0151 708 0117
Research tel: 0151 708 0136

Contents

Foreword

Where would this country be without charity? The United Kingdom, few seem to realise, is now the most centralised, business-dominated entity in the democratic world. The continued decline in adhesion to any faith or other value system, and to communalism, makes the world of charity an evermore indispensable repository for individual and collective altruism and engagement.

That was why, assisted by Keith Smith, I was originally prompted to write this handbook. The object was – and still is – to minimise the burden of charity law for charity trustees by giving them plain English, practical, astute advice.

That is also why I am delighted with the new team – Julian Blake, Alice Faure Walker and Christine Rigby – who are carrying that purpose forward. I could not want for a better trio given their deep experience of charity law in practice and their personal commitment to the sector as well as the aims of the handbook.

I thank them and everyone else at Bates Wells and Braithwaite who have contributed to this sixth edition, which, in particular, incorporates the major reforms of the Charities Act 2006. The handbook could not be in better hands.

As always, I doff my hat to that majority of my fellow citizens who actively sustain the wondrous world of charity.

Andrew Phillips
Bates Wells and Braithwaite
January 2008

Preface

Operating a charity has become a much bigger subject in the 27 plus years since the first edition of this handbook. We have seen 'the professionalisation of the sector'; the 'contract culture'; the growth of the Charity Commission from essentially a registrar into a highly influential sectoral regulator; two major statutes (in 1992/3 and 2006); a plethora of administrative reforms and the challenges and opportunities of the outsourcing of major public services and the social enterprise movement. During this time the sector itself has expanded at a rapid and consistent rate so, at this moment, there are more than 168,000 main registered charities, with many thousands of other voluntary and community organisations operating, whether knowingly or not, on a charitable basis.

During all these developments, the core principles of charitable status have remained essentially the same: a UK organisation is a charity if it has exclusively public benefit purposes and activities and if it applies all its assets, including any surpluses (or profits) to its purposes and not to benefit those involved in the organisation's operation. If an organisation is a charity it must (unless specifically excepted) register with the Charity Commission in England and Wales, or the equivalents in Scotland and Northern Ireland and must be accountable for its public benefit operation. A charity is entitled to significant tax advantages and has a brand identity which generates an extremely high level of public support and goodwill.

This sixth edition is, therefore, very much an updating of its predecessors: it provides the same straightforward explanations of what a charity is and how it should operate, while placing that information in its much changed context. Above all, it is intended to provide the same practical and necessary information, for the same dedicated and worthy audience as ever – the vast and infinitely varied citizens' army that is the UK's voluntary and community sector.

No individual has done more in this cause than the original author of this handbook, Andrew Phillips. As the founder of a new London-based firm of solicitors in 1970, Andrew applied the traditional socially engaged approach of the local solicitor to the national scene and invented the concept of the charity law practice as a self-contained discipline. This culminated in his leading contribution to the parliamentary debates on the Charities Act 2006 as Lord Phillips of Sudbury. I am privileged to have learned my trade at his knee and now to be one of over 30 members of the Charity and Social Enterprise Department at Bates Wells and Braithwaite, the firm that

Andrew created. I am also privileged to be his successor as the principal author of this seminal charity law publication, though the key to the firm and the handbook is that, to Andrew and to the many who have learnt from him, law, and especially charity law, is a practical subject, or it is nothing.

I am very grateful also, to colleagues at Bates Wells and Braithwaite, who have contributed to this edition, most especially Christine Rigby and Alice Faure Walker, who would properly be credited as my co-authors and also to Bill Lewis, Stephanie Biden and Rosamund McCarthy.

We are all deeply grateful for the support we have received from the Directory of Social Change over six editions of the handbook and particularly, in relation to this edition, John Martin and Lucy Muir-Smith, and to our editor Jacki Reason.

Julian Blake
Bates Wells and Braithwaite
January 2008

1 New charity law in 2006

The Charities Act 2006, applicable in England and Wales and coming into force over a period of several years from November 2006, will broadly reclassify the traditional four categories of charity, with some extensions and updating, into thirteen, and provide a range of other modernising provisions which will make life easier for organisations and individuals working across the spectrum of charitable activity. A high profile public debate about whether independent schools and private hospitals should retain their charitable status resulted in mild reform, avoiding any radical legal change but heightening regulatory scrutiny.

Scotland acquired its own charity legislation in the Charities and Trustee Investment (Scotland) Act 2005. This established the Office of the Scottish Charity Regulator (OSCR) as an independent regulator north of the border and marks some divergence in the definition of 'charity' and the regulatory approach from those applicable in England and Wales

Northern Ireland is to follow suit in developing its own charity law and establishing its own Charity Commission of Northern Ireland (to be known as CCNI) during 2008.

For the purposes of this Handbook, dedicated to the practical, the fundamentals of charity law and most of the well-established principles and practices remain unchanged, and in this sixth edition they are placed in the new regulatory context.

It should be emphasised, though, that the Handbook deals predominantly with the position in England and Wales and not the separate legal jurisdictions of Scotland and Northern Ireland.

2 Why establish a charity?

2.1 The charitable sector

There are well over 500,000 UK charities. In June 2007 just over 190,000 were registered with the Charity Commission and this number was increasing by around 5,000 a year. The number of registered charities will increase significantly in 2008/09 when parts of the Charities Act 2006 come into force, requiring some of the previously exempt or excepted types of charity (such as universities) to register for the first time. At the same time, the Charity Commission is becoming more rigorous about ensuring charities that have become inactive are de-registered and that the charitable nature of registered charities is reviewed more systematically.

The charitable sector is still marvellously independent and diverse, a constant in everyday community life and an ever more important force in public policy and the national economy. Most charities start and remain small, but some grow to become household names. Others combine as federations of separately registered charities, as is the case with Citizens' Advice Bureaux and Women's Institutes. The great majority are community based, have no paid staff, and are particularly hard hit by extra bureaucracy.

Why do people go to the considerable trouble and (usually) expense of seeking charitable status?

2.2 Benefits of charitable status

Public recognition and support

Above all, in a sceptical age the public will be greatly reassured if your organisation is a charity. Despite the tiny number of highly publicised fraudsters, the word 'charity' continues to evoke a very positive response in most people. If you have to rely on public support, being able to say 'we are a charity' is almost indispensable. Equally important is the opportunity to make funding requests of grant-giving bodies, most of which are charitable foundations. They, like the public, are bombarded with requests for money. Some are prevented by their constitutions from making grants to non-charities, and many more are inclined to operate an internal rule of thumb, excluding non-charitable applicants. The same can apply to public authority funding. This first winnowing may be crude, but it is a fact of life.

Eligibility for a grant from the Big Lottery Fund is dependent on the applicant being a 'charitable, philanthropic or benevolent organisation'. The vast majority of applicants are charitable, and the definitions of philanthropic and benevolent are only very narrowly different.

Volunteers

Although there has been a steady increase in the number of paid staff in the charity sector, it is still underpinned by the traditional legions of volunteers. They exemplify what the public perceives as 'charitable', and undertake a multitude of functions for the charities they support, from acting as trustees (over a million), through helping with office administration and fundraising, to helping at the village fête (and often all of these). Without the magic word 'charity' it is far more difficult to get volunteers.

Tax benefits

The tax benefits for charities have steadily increased over the last 25 years and charities and donors get added satisfaction through the gift aid scheme (see below), which increases donations by diverting tax payments to the recipient charity. Charities in the UK probably enjoy the most generous tax regime in the world. The benefits include:

- income/corporation tax – not payable by charities on donations, rental income or surplus from business operations in pursuit of charitable objects – 'primary purpose' profits (see 11.3);
- gift aid on donations by individual taxpayers – the charity may reclaim the basic rate tax attributable to the income donated and the taxpayer may reclaim any higher rate element (see 12.1);
- gift aid on donations by UK companies – the company may deduct a gift as a charge on income from taxable profit (see 12.1);
- business rates – charities are exempt from 80% of the charge and may benefit from further relief, up to 100%, depending on local authority policy (see 12.2);
- stamp duty land tax on real property and stamp duty on shares – not payable by charities (see 12.2);
- inheritance tax – not payable from estates on gifts to charities on, or within seven years before, death (see 12.1);
- capital gains tax – not payable by donors on gifts to charity, or by charities on disposals (see 12.1);

- value added tax – some provisions are linked to goods and services provided by charities and some to not-for-profit operation – the rules are particularly detailed (see 12.2).

The taxation system is nonetheless complex, has changed rapidly in recent years and remains subject to change, particularly in annual Finance Acts (see chapter 12).

2.3   Possible disadvantages of becoming a charity

- Charity law imposes high standards of stewardship (see chapters 8 and 9).
- As public benefit organisations, charities are subject to a corresponding level of regulation and the bureaucracy that comes with it (see chapter 10).
- The general rule against charity trustees benefiting personally from their charity precludes (subject to limited exceptions) board of management members being paid (but see 8.5).
- Trading activities will be restricted to those pursuing the relevant charitable purposes or, subject to limited exceptions, those undertaken though a separate trading arm (see chapter 11).
- A charity may not undertake partisan political activity and campaigning (as distinct from activities in pursuit of its objects touching the political sphere) (see chapter 13).

3 Legal advice

3.1 When?

Charities need lawyers and other professionals more now than in the past, though there is still a healthy tradition of charities 'doing their own thing' as far as possible. Lawyers can be expensive, and only a few have substantial experience of charity law. Nonetheless, in the modern regulatory climate, there comes a time to seek advice, and a charity can harm itself by not so doing. Not properly understanding corporate/ unincorporated status, constitutional structure, basic charity law requirements or restrictions on trading can store up serious problems, and not taking advice on drafting charity objects and describing proposed activities can cause unnecessary difficulties in seeking to register a charity.

3.2 Who?

If your proposed charity is following a well-worn path, and a relevant constitutional model (whether one of the Charity Commission's or one used by another organisation in your field) really does fit, then use it.

Otherwise, find a solicitor who is reasonably experienced in handling charity formations of the kind with which you are involved. Seek recommendations from informed sources – other charities in the same field, grant-giving foundations, advisory services and (perhaps best of all) from solicitors you may know.

3.3 Cost

If you can get good, free ('pro bono') advice, then so much the better. Otherwise, the tendency of many organisations is to skimp setting-up costs, if only because, until they are registered, they may be extremely hard up. However, this can prove to be a false economy.

An inexperienced solicitor will tend to give inexperienced advice which, with a difficult registration, can lead to delay and rebuff, lost time and expense and having to start again. This can create real problems.

The able solicitor, with wide experience, may quote a higher rate or fee, but end up being cheaper, quicker and better. Always ask for an overall estimate. Unless the work is open-ended, it should be possible to provide this. The true charity law solicitor will, however, be recognisable by being appropriately cost sensitive.

OUR CHARITY RATES... YES, THEY VARY WITH THE THICKNESS OF THE CARPET PILE AND THE PLENITUDE OF MARBLE

3.4   A good service

At your first meeting with solicitors, you should ask about their experience of your kind of work, and whether they foresee obstacles to registration. Are they, for example, going to use a model objects clause and model constitution?

You should also establish the priority they can give your work and roughly how long they expect each stage of the formation and registration to take.

Crucially, you will need astute advice on the appropriate constitutional form for your charity, particularly if there is to be a membership, branches or non-standard governance arrangements. Many refinements can safely be left for future decision.

Note that asking a solicitor to work from your preliminary draft constitution will usually increase, rather than save, costs.

3.5 How?

It is important to instruct a solicitor in whom you have confidence and with whom you can get along. Trust him or her to do a reasonable job in a fair way. Most solicitors respond best to that. If you do not clearly understand anything ask for clarification; if matters then remain obscure you are probably not getting the best advice. If you have a query or complaint, get it off your chest in a civil way. Don't let things fester.

Even if it seems appropriate for you simply to take over another charity's constitution lock, stock and barrel, it may still be advantageous to work with and through a solicitor, as differences in circumstances may not be apparent to the untrained eye.

3.6 Other assistance

There are several agencies that are experienced in advising groups how to register, such as the National Council for Voluntary Organisations (NCVO) and the National Housing Federation (NHF) (see appendix 1). Others may be active in your particular field, so ask.

You should certainly obtain a copy of the constitution of other charities operating in your field. This can serve as a guide to you and your solicitor or adviser. Copies of any charity's constitution can be obtained by submitting a written request to the Charity Commission, or you could simply contact the other charities directly. Key information about registered charities (such as type of constitution and main objects) are accessible at www.charitycommission.gov.uk.

3.7 Timing

The time from submitting a completed application to the Charity Commission to formal registration varies a great deal. A routine application efficiently handled by the Commission may take only a few weeks; more difficult or unconventional cases (and the less well handled) can take many months. The most problematic can take years.

If authentically urgent circumstances arise, the Commission will usually try to help.

4 What is charitable?

A charity is not simply an organisation dedicated to doing things that may be considered worthy or worthwhile. As you might expect, there are legal constraints that must be adhered to and complied with.

Roughly speaking there is a four-prong test:

1   The organisation must be established on a 'not-for-profit' basis – see 4.1.
2   The formally stated objects or purposes of the charity must fall within one of 13 broad categories of charitable purpose – see 4.2 and chapter 5.
3   The objects must be exclusively charitable – see 4.3.
4   The charity must operate for the public benefit – see 4.4.

The general principles are explained below. Chapter 5 looks in more detail at the 13 broad charitable purposes and how they fit with modern types of charity.

4.1   Not-for-profit

Not-for-profit does not mean that the organisation should not make a profit from its operations. What it means is that any profits made should not be distributed (for example to members or trustees) but should be reinvested

in the organisation. For more on how these restrictions are built in to a charity's constitution, see chapter 6.

4.2   Charitable purposes

The Charities Act 2006 (2006 Act) sets out, for the first time, a definition of 13 categories of charity. The relevant parts of the Act came into force on 1 April 2008.

This categorisation broadly updates previous 'common law' (legal development, through custom and judicial decision), based on an original statement of charitable purposes in a 1601 Act of Parliament. That statement evolved over time into the following four categories (or 'heads') of charity:

- relief of poverty;
- advancement of education;
- promotion of religion;
- other purposes beneficial to the community in a way recognised as charitable (known as 'the fourth head').

The new list of 13 charitable categories (in England and Wales) is:

(a)   The prevention or relief of poverty (see 5.1).

(b)   The advancement of education (see 5.2).

(c)   The advancement of religion (see 5.3).

(d)   The advancement of health or the saving of lives (see 5.4).

(e)   The advancement of citizenship or community development (see 5.5).

(f)   The advancement of the arts, culture, heritage or science (see 5.6).

(g)   The advancement of amateur sport (see 5.7).

(h)   The advancement of human rights, conflict resolution or reconciliation or the promotion of religious or racial harmony or equality and diversity (see 5.8).

(i)   The advancement of environmental protection or improvement (see 5.9).

(j)   The relief of those in need by reason of youth, age, ill-health, disability, financial hardship or other disadvantage (see 5.10).

(k)   The advancement of animal welfare (see 5.11).

(l)   The promotion of the efficiency of the armed forces of the Crown, or of the efficiency of the police, fire and rescue services or ambulance services (see 5.12).

(m) Any other purposes accepted as charitable on the day that this part of the Act comes into force, and any purpose that is analogous to or within the spirit of any of the purposes listed in the Act or accepted as charitable after the new law comes into force (see 5.13).

The three previous specific categories are therefore repeated as purposes (a) to (c), with clarification that prevention as well as relief of poverty is charitable. The general previous fourth category is repeated as purpose (m), with an explicit statement indicating the intent that the definition of charity will continue to evolve in the way it has to date, through new purposes being recognised within the intent of the original 1601 purposes, or now the 2006 Act, updated to the modern setting. The nine new categories were carved out of purposes already more or less firmly established and recognised by the Charity Commission, in 2006, as being within the previous general fourth category.

All purposes previously recognised as charitable under English and Welsh law will continue to be charitable once the new provisions of the Charities Act 2006 come into force. Case law up to 2006 will continue to have application in interpreting the extent of the 13 categories.

For more detail and examples of charities falling within each of the categories, see chapter 5.

4.3   Requirement for exclusively charitable objects

The objectives/goals/aims/ends for which any charity exists are set out in what is called the 'objects' or 'purposes' clause in its constitution. This clause is typically followed by a 'powers' clause, setting out the means the charity may use to achieve its objects.

The objects clause is the foundation stone of a charity and the definition of its legal scope of activity. Any action outside the objects is unauthorised and unlawful (or, as traditional lawyers say, ultra vires). If charity trustees allow expenditure on activity not within the objects or not authorised by the powers, they are in breach of duty and vulnerable to being held personally liable to reimburse the charity (see chapter 9).

A charity's objects must be exclusively charitable. This means they must fall exclusively within one or more of the 13 charitable categories (including the general 13th) on any sensible reading of the words used.

Occasionally this gives rise to difficulties. This was vividly illustrated by a case where the court held that 'charitable and deserving' purposes were exclusively charitable – 'and' having the effect of the narrowing the scope of 'charitable' – whereas 'charitable or deserving' purposes were not – 'or' having the effect of extending the scope of 'charitable'.

Inexpertly drafted charitable objects sometimes include a list of proposed purposes, with one purpose, or part of a purpose, inadvertently extending the objects beyond what is charitable. This is fatal to charitable status (though the solution may be to remove the offending clause by constitutional amendment).

The Charity Commission website has some examples of model objects clauses for common types of charities. It can also be useful to search via the Commission website for charities carrying out similar activities to those you propose – you can search the Register of Charities either by reference to known names or key words. The objects of those charities will give you some ideas on wording that the Commission has accepted as charitable.

Expert, or at least well-informed, drafting is also extremely important in ensuring that your objects strike the right balance between describing what you intend to do, within the scope of defined categories of charity, while retaining suitable flexibility for future development. Simply by reciting one or more of the 13 categories of charitable activity will not usually be sufficient to fulfil the drafting exercise.

4.4　Public benefit

What is it?

Charity law requires charities to be of an essentially altruistic character and therefore in this sense they are, by definition, public benefit organisations. This is often expressed by saying that a charity must be capable of benefiting the whole community, or a substantial section of it. This tends to rule out clubs dedicated to members' personal interests, unless they have open membership as well as exclusively charitable objects. However, restrictions on membership are acceptable if they are function-related, for example, a geographical restriction may limit benefit to inhabitants of a village.

It is also clear that 'substantial' in this context can be relative. For example, a charity to research a rare disease would not be ruled out because there are only a few actual and potential sufferers. In contrast, an appeal confined to a named individual for medical treatment could not be 'for public benefit' and a charitable one.

A charity in any category may have objects that extend to activity abroad, so the 'public' is not to be read as limited to the UK public.

Incidental private benefit

Private benefit is death to charity if it is part of an organisation's objects, but where it is an unavoidable consequence of the charitable work and is 'incidental and ancillary' to the predominant public benefit, it will, generally, be acceptable. This can need particular assessment and perhaps the adjustment of projects. For example, charitable regeneration projects will usually have some level of beneficial impact on community members who would not be considered to be disadvantaged, and a judgment needs to be made about the extent to which identified 'private benefit' may properly be considered incidental and ancillary.

The public benefit test in England and Wales

So an organisation is charitable if it is established exclusively for one or more of the 13 purposes, on a not-for-profit basis and is 'for the public benefit'.

Before the 2006 Act there was a legal presumption that not-for-profit organisations with charitable purposes to relieve poverty, advance education or promote religion were 'for the public benefit'. However, in a provision of the Act that primarily arose out of debate on the established charitable status of independent schools and private hospitals, this presumption will no longer apply, and public benefit must be actively demonstrated in each case.

There was extensive debate in relation to the 2006 Act as to whether it should contain any legal definition of 'public benefit'; the conclusion was that it should not. As periodic reviews in the UK and a number of other countries have found, it is nearly impossible to provide a definition that both provides a precise test of public benefit and can change with time. Where statutory definitions do exist, as in Scotland (see 4.5), they remain in essence a statement of interpretation principles.

This means that previous law on what 'public benefit' means will apply, with the proviso that there is scope for, in essence, revised interpretation. What this will mean in practice depends on how the Charity Commission undertakes its regulatory functions, subject to constraint by the Charity Tribunal (a creation of the 2006 Act) and ultimately the High Court.

The 2006 Act requires the Charity Commission to issue guidance promoting awareness and understanding of the meaning of 'public benefit', with such consultation as it considers appropriate. The Commission carried out an initial consultation process in early 2007 and published the final version of its public benefit guidance, *Charities and public benefit*, in January 2008. Further guidance for six specific sub-sectors will be published later in 2008, after consultation. The six sub-sectors are: educational charities, religious charities, charities charging fees, charities for the relief of poverty, charities promoting social inclusion and non-religious belief charities.

The guidance sets out two key principles of public benefit the Charity Commission will apply to new and existing charities. Within each principle there are some important factors that must be considered in all cases.

Principle 1:		There must be an identifiable benefit or benefits.
	1a	It must be clear what the benefits are.
	1b	The benefits must be related to the aims.
	1c	The benefits must be balanced against any detriment or harm.
Principle 2:		Benefit must be to the public or section of the public
	2a	The beneficiaries must be appropriate to the aims.
	2b	Where benefit is to a section of the public, the opportunity to benefit must not be unreasonably restricted:
		- by geographical or other restrictions; or
		- by ability to pay any fees charged.
	2c	People in poverty must not be excluded from the opportunity to benefit.
	2d	Any private benefits must be incidental.

Principle 2c was the most contentious, being derived from the debate on fee charging. The guidance gives examples of ways to ensure people in poverty are not excluded from the opportunity to benefit. They include not just offering lower fees but also sharing the charity's resources in other ways, such as an independent school working in partnership with a local state school or an arts charity broadcasting operatic performances to a wider audience via TV or radio. That said, there is no doubt that fee charging charities will be obliged to demonstrate public benefit actively in a way that was not directly required before the 2006 Act. The specific sub-sector guidance for fee earning charities expected later in 2008 will shed more light on this, as will case by case interpretation. However, there is certainly a danger for law and Charity Commission guidance/policy to be seen as the same thing. The 2006 Act did not change the law and much of the analysis surrounding public benefit and fee-charging remains open to question and scrutiny. This is an area where specialist advice may be essential.

The guidance elaborates on both principles in more detail. It also sets out the requirement for trustees to include a statement of how the charity has delivered public benefit in the annual trustees' report.

What if the Commission takes the view that an existing charity is failing to deliver sufficient public benefit? The guidance explains the steps the Commission will take, the emphasis being on working with charities and giving them time to adjust to the new requirement. At worst, the Commission has powers to alter the charity's purposes or enforce change by using its regulatory powers.

It is also important to be clear about the effect of an assessment that an organisation previously considered charitable is not engaging in charitable activities. The 2006 Act itself is not precise on this but, in accordance with charity law principle, technically there is no such thing as 'a charity ceasing to be charitable'. Instead, one of the following circumstances might apply:

- A registered charity is no longer able to fulfil its original charitable purposes. The solution would be for the Charity Commission to exercise its powers to allow the assets of the charity to be applied to other charitable purposes as similar as possible to the original ones.
- A registered charity established for charitable purposes is found not to be engaging in exclusively charitable activities within those purposes. The solution would be for the trustees of the charity (or the Charity Commission, using powers of intervention) to change the activities to ensure that they match the established charitable purposes.
- A registered charity is considered not to have charitable purposes. One solution could be for the Charity Commission to recognise original charitable intent and for the charity to amend its purposes to reflect that. If that were not possible the Commission would have to acknowledge that registration was in error. This would mean a) that a

charity would have benefited, in error, from charitable tax privileges, and b) that assets thought to have been irrevocably dedicated to the public benefit had not been and therefore, potentially, they would be distributable to private interests.

- The law changes to make something that was once charitable, non-charitable. If this was statutory, the relevant act should really address the consequences. If it is a matter of modernising interpretation such consequences would stand to be addressed by the Charity Commission. This situation arose in relation to gun clubs, which in 1911 were thought to be charitable on the basis that they assisted the defence of the realm. In the 1990s this rationale was deemed no longer applicable. However, the logic of this was not followed through to assist with future interpretations as to how to deal with the change in tax status, or the change in the dedication of assets to the public benefit.

4.5   The public benefit test in Scotland and Northern Ireland

Charity law in Scotland (by virtue of the Charities and Trustee Investment (Scotland) Act 2005) provides a similar but not identical definition of charitable purposes and public benefit. This sets up the potential for the divergence of charity law in Scotland and charity law in England and Wales.

The list of categories of what is regarded as charitable in Scotland differs slightly in relation to religious and sports related charities. There is also a more explicitly defined public benefit test under which regard must be had to private benefit and 'disbenefit' to the public, compared with benefit to the public, and to 'whether any condition on obtaining benefit (including any charge or fee) is unduly restrictive'.

The intention and likely effect look similar to the new law in England and Wales, but the fact is that different statutory provisions have been introduced in the different countries and there is scope for different legal interpretations to follow from this.

Similarly in Northern Ireland, under legislation expected in 2008, the list of categories of what is regarded as charitable is expected to be slightly different, so that the advancement of peace and community relations are expressly stated to be charitable purposes. The public benefit test is more similar to the Scottish than to the English test.

The result is that there is the potential for subtly different charity law in each of the three legal jurisdictions of the UK.

5 The categories of charity

5.1 Charitable category (a) – the prevention and relief of poverty

There is no neat definition of 'poverty', but it is probably the most obviously identifiable charitable purpose and only really requires interpretation in relation to schemes where cause and effect are not direct and need explanation. Also, in its charitable sense, the definition is relative and generous. All those in receipt of means-tested benefits are virtually certain to be charitably 'poor'. But so, too, may be individuals who would not qualify for state support but who, compared with their previous lifestyle and expectations, have fallen on relatively hard times. For example, all the professions have their benevolent funds. At the time of writing, the Charity Commission has suggested that this interpretation may be outdated, but that view is likely to be resisted.

It is well established that, for 'relief of poverty' charities, there is a general public benefit in providing for the relief of a smaller defined beneficiary group than would be sufficient to demonstrate public benefit in a different charitable category. For example, a trust to relieve the poverty of the ex-employees of one business may be charitable, whereas a similar trust to educate the children of the same group would not meet the public benefit test. Specific guidance from the Charity Commission on how the public benefit test applies to relief of poverty charities (see chapter 4) is expected sometime in late 2008, after consultation.

It is now express law that 'prevention' as well as 'relief' of poverty is a charitable purpose. In the past there were, occasionally, some frustratingly literal interpretations of 'relief' suggesting, against reason, that the equally desirable social purpose of preventing poverty in the first place was not charitable. 'Micro-credit' (credit or banking facilities for those who are not conventionally considered creditworthy) is increasingly important in promoting the entrepreneurial self-help route out of poverty, particularly abroad.

Charitable purpose (j), relating to the relief of other specific types of disadvantage and hardship (traditionally the 'aged, sick and impotent') was, before the Charities Act 2006 (2006 Act), sometimes considered to be an application of the 'relief of poverty' category and sometimes within the fourth general category ('other purposes beneficial to the community in a way recognised as charitable').

Charitable relief of poverty may be achieved by indirect means. This could be, for example, by providing travel facilities to enable hard-up relatives of prisoners to visit them, or the cost of a holiday to relieve a struggling family. Also see 'Relief of unemployment', below.

'Relief of poverty' objects

There is a modern preference for avoiding the starkness of the word 'poverty' in drafting objects and using instead terms without the distasteful connotation of underclass. For example, 'in hardship', 'disadvantaged', 'in need', 'of moderate or limited means', 'not self-supporting' and similar expressions are acceptable. A modern language version of 'The object of the charity is the relief of poverty' usually needs no further elaboration except, perhaps, to add specific reference to a beneficiary group and/or to principal intended methods for achieving relief. More specific types of charity related to this category include the following.

Relief of unemployment

A Charity Commission guidance leaflet (RR3: *Charities and the Relief of Unemployment*:) sets out considerations relating to this application of the 'relief of poverty' category (though relief of unemployment is also treated as within the catch-all category (m) – see below) and sets out specific model objects clauses and activities that (generally) the Commission considers may and may not be undertaken in relation to such objects. For example, the following are accepted as charitable:

- Advice and training concerning employment, self employment, co-ops, CV writing, job search and job club facilities.
- Practical support such as accommodation, childcare facilities or assistance with travel.
- Provision of capital grants, loans, equipment and premises free or at below market rates for start-ups.
- Subsidy to an existing business to take on unemployed people.

Relief of poverty by the promotion of urban and rural regeneration

This overlaps with category (e) – see below for more on this.

Relief of poverty by fair trade

Problems, firstly of tracking real benefit back to the poor producers, and secondly of ancillary private advantage (e.g. to UK supermarkets selling fair-traded products), prevented registration of a fair trade charity until 1995, when the Fairtrade Foundation was at last accepted. The Foundation is obliged to monitor delivery of the benefits to poor producers, which includes ongoing assessments to see whether the beneficiaries are still within the scheme's charitable criteria.

As a later extension of this principle, shops run directly by charities can now major in selling new fair trade goods, rather than donated goods.

For sources of further information see 5.15.

5.2 Charitable category (b) – the advancement of education

Historically, this category was widely interpreted to allow registration for a whole range of organisations advancing education in all sorts of fields, e.g. the arts, research and some sports. While that is still possible under the 2006 Act, many of these types of organisations are more likely to register under some of the more specific newly defined categories – see 5.6 and 5.7.

Nevertheless, this remains a cornerstone of what is a charitable purpose and, as with 'poverty', there is no hard and fast definition, though a demonstration of genuine educational merit is required. In practice, so long as a well-reasoned and supported case can be made to the Charity Commission, new branches of teaching, learning and research should be acceptable for charitable status.

Information v education

Requisite educational merit must be contrasted with the 'mere provision of information'. For this reason it is desirable, where doubt might arise, to back up a relevant application with authoritative support that places it within the generally acknowledged educational sphere.

Propaganda v education

In one case, objects 'for the public to be educated to an acceptance that peace is best secured by demilitarisation' were found by the High Court not to be charitable. So, too, an organisation to propagate the views of a particular person, party or movement will be barred from charitable status (other than in relation to a religion), because a court will not be competent to judge whether the propounded views, values or policies are in the public interest. Study of the philosophy, life and work of an esteemed historical figure will, by contrast, be admissible.

Business education v consultancy

The promotion of business education has long been looked upon as charitable, as has the teaching of technical and professional skills. There is a distinction, however, between general education and training on the one hand and bespoke advice or consultancy on the other. The latter will not be charitable unless it is to or for a charity or a class of charitable beneficiaries.

Political education

The courts have long disallowed as charities organisations they consider propagandist or committed to a particular doctrine, party or movement. They do, however, accept that education about politics in an academic way is acceptable, as is education in political principles. Political think tanks often steer a fine line in this regard (see 13.6).

In practice, success or failure in an application for registration on the edge of politics may depend to a great extent on the confidence the Charity Commission has in the integrity of the applicants, the proposed trustees and their preparatory work (see chapter 13).

Education and public benefit

All educational charities now have to demonstrate how they benefit the public. In many cases, this will be straightforward, but there are two specific issues to note:

- **Non-beneficial education** – occasionally education is not 'beneficial'. Such was the bequest of George Bernard Shaw to fund development of a new alphabet. The court thought it so eccentric as to lack the necessary public benefit.

- **Fee charging charities** – the issue of whether private schools which charge high fees should retain their charitable status was not addressed directly in the 2006 Act – instead it has been left to the Charity Commission to issue guidance on how such charities must demonstrate public benefit. In the guidance on public benefit (see 4.4), the Charity Commission makes clear that any argument based on 'relieving the public purse' (i.e. that by the charity providing its services, it is taking people out of the government funded systems) will not on its own be sufficient to demonstrate public benefit.

The most relevant of the public benefit principles set out by the Commission in its guidance is principle 2c 'people in poverty must not be excluded from the opportunity to benefit'. This means, at least, that a charity cannot be set up so that either constitutionally or in practice (because of the level of fees) people in poverty are definitely excluded. Having said that, the guidance states that the fact services are provided mainly to people who can afford to pay does not necessarily mean that the organisation is not set up for the public benefit.

So for private schools, while some outside markers have been laid down for what is and is not sufficient to demonstrate public benefit, the Commission has yet to come off the fence and set quantifiable targets that they must meet. The specific sub-sector guidance for charities that charge fees (due to

be issued later in 2008) should assist with this, although it seems likely that for some time to come the only way to judge matters authoritatively will be on a case by case basis. The Commission's website is the best place to look for the latest guidance – see 5.15. Remember again that the Commission is the fount of guidance on the established (and to a significant extent still unclear) law and is not itself the definitive source of law.

5.3   Charitable category (c) – the advancement of religion

Prior to the 2006 Act, the registration of religious organisations as charities was not always straightforward. Single deity faiths were generally OK, but multi deity faiths, in some cases, had to register either as educational organisations advancing the teachings of a particular faith or under the 'fourth head' as being otherwise 'beneficial to the community', through 'promoting the moral and spiritual welfare and improvement of the community'. Similarly many non-deity and humanist faiths had to register under the 'fourth head'.

The most detailed examination of whether a particular system of beliefs qualified as a religion came in the Commissioners' decision (1999) refusing to register the Church of Scientology as a charity. The decision states that to be a religion there must be:

- a belief in a Supreme Being;
- expression of that belief through worship of the Supreme Being;
- advancement of the religion by the organisation;
- benefit to the public.

Against this background, the 2006 Act bravely introduces a clarification of what 'religion' includes – 'belief in more than one god' and 'a religion which does not involve belief in a god'. As you might expect, this was the subject of much debate as the Bill proceeded through Parliament, with the government asserting that this would not fundamentally change the definition of religion applied by the Commission.

The 2006 Act does not override existing case law, so the partial definition of 'religion' set out in the Act sits alongside the Scientology case.

Merits of a religion

The Unification Church (alias the Moonies) was registered by the Charity Commission on the grounds that it was not the Commission's role to evaluate the relative merits of a new religion as compared with an established one. Public outcry against the Moonies' perceived (or perhaps assumed) practices led to a rare appeal by the Attorney General against the Commission in the High Court to have the registration withdrawn. That appeal did not proceed for want of evidence, and the registration stands.

Lifestyle organisations v religion

The proliferation of 'new-age' and other organisations with a defining spiritual purpose, but only a peripheral identification with established religion, will continue to raise difficult interpretative issues. Some will be able to show an historical religious pedigree (e.g. some yogic organisations) and some may be accepted within category (m). Others may be rejected as being 'mere lifestyle organisations' and so not beneficial to the public in a charitable sense. Much depends on the quality of submissions for charitable status in this category. The guidance being prepared by the Commission on public benefit and religious charities considers the degree of cogency that a belief system must have to be recognised as a religion. This is likely to require an element of worship or reverence.

Public benefit

In a case in 1949 the court decided that a gift for an order of enclosed, contemplative nuns was not charitable because, although plainly a religious order, it lacked that public outreach or benefit (in this case instruction or edification of the public) which is essential. The court declared itself unable to accept the public efficacy of the nuns' prayers. Semi-enclosed orders have a similar problem.

The removal of the presumption of public benefit (see 4.4) has caused particular concern to religious charities. During the passage of the Charities Bill through parliament, religious charities received any number of assurances that they had nothing to fear from the new legislation. However, in the draft guidance on public benefit issued in 2007, the Charity Commission cited religious charities as being at risk of not being able to demonstrate public benefit. This led to a staggering two-thirds (500 plus) of responses to the Commission's consultation coming from religious organisations, demonstrating the depth of concern in the sector.

The Commission is expected to produce specific sub-sector guidance for religious charities in the course of 2008 – its website is the best place to check the latest guidance. The general message remains a reassuring one.

Places of worship

Note that many registered religious places of worship and their congregations, though charitable, are exempt from registration (see 7.4) and therefore are not required to register with the Charity Commission.

For sources of further guidance see 5.15.

5.4 Charitable category (d) – the advancement of health or the saving of lives

The first of the 'new' categories, this is specifically stated to include the prevention or relief of sickness, disease or human suffering. It would, for example, cover a traditional medical research charity or a hospital, and also organisations offering complementary or alternative therapies.

The Commission states that, to be charitable, there needs to be sufficient efficacy of the method to be used. That is straightforward with regard to organisations practising well-accepted activities such as acupuncture, osteopathy or faith-healing, but will be more demanding of those practising new or less well-known forms of treatment. The field is still developing in relation to spiritual practices outside the framework of an established religion.

Evidence could take the form of case studies (including from abroad) or rest on the fact that the treatment or therapy is acceptable to a significant section of the mainstream 'medical profession'.

There is an overlap between this category and categories (j) and (l) – see below.

For sources of further guidance see 5.15.

5.5 Charitable category (e) – the advancement of citizenship or community development

The Act clarifies that this category includes:

(i)   rural or urban regeneration;
(ii) the promotion of civic responsibility, volunteering, the voluntary sector or the effectiveness or efficiency of charities.

So it would include charities to promote volunteering or to support other charities, organisations which promote civic responsibility and good citizenship and organisations regenerating particular geographical areas.

Community development

A community development organisation is distinguishable from a community organisation as the specific purpose of the former is developing the community's capacity for self-help. The Commission recommends objects along the following lines:

> To develop the capacity and skills of the members of the [socially and economically] [socially] disadvantaged community of [...] in such a way that they are better able to identify, and help meet, their needs and to participate more fully in society.

Note that the community need not necessarily be a geographical one (the Commission also accepts there can be a 'community of interest'). Private benefit is also to be watched – see 4.4.

Regeneration

The Commission guidelines on regeneration endorse the following activities to benefit those in need:

- financial or other assistance;
- housing and provision improvement;
- help in finding employment;
- education, training and work experience;
- assistance to new or existing businesses to provide training and employment;
- the preservation of historic buildings;
- provision of public amenities.

The guidance (RR2: *Promotion of Urban and Rural Regeneration*) also gives examples of objects that could appear in the governing document of a regeneration charity.

The Charity Commission, in line with its 'gateway' policy (see 7.7), stipulates that a regeneration charity will normally need to demonstrate that:

- it has effective criteria to determine whether an area is in need of regeneration;
- its activities will cover a broad spectrum of regeneration work;
- the public benefit from its activities will outweigh any incidental private benefit – see 4.4;
- the organisation will measure the benefits provided.

Note the potential overlap between activities of regeneration charities and those of local authorities. The Charity Commission generally takes the view that it is acceptable to supplement statutory funding, but not to substitute for it. That may be wrong in law and is not as clear a distinction as it might appear.

For sources of further guidance see 5.15.

5.6   Charitable category (f) – the advancement of the arts, culture, heritage or science

Previously charities carrying out these activities did so mainly under the head of 'advancement of education'. This new category includes promoting various forms of art at national/professional and local/amateur level. The subject matter has to pass an 'objective' test of artistic merit applied by the Commission – in one case that went to court the judge described a proposed artistic collection as no more than 'foisting a mass of junk upon the public'. Community arts organisations such as street theatre groups are acceptable provided they do not have a politically propagandist agenda.

However, whereas 'cultural' or 'classical' objects have generally proved acceptable, 'mere entertainment' or 'artistic purposes' have been held by the courts to be too wide and vague to be charitable. These distinctions are bemusing and can only be understood (if at all) in context and in the light of the patchy evolution of case law, inhibited as it has been by the wholly inadequate and unschematic flow of cases to the High Court (see 7.10).

Two particular public benefit issues can arise for charities in this category:

* Charities that charge high fees (such as an opera house or theatre) must be able to demonstrate that the poor are not excluded from the opportunity to benefit – see chapter 4.
* While research activities are generally charitable, to be of public benefit the useful results must be made available to the public by publication or on a come-and-get-it basis. Thus a charity doing sponsored research which precludes, or unduly delays, such access will fail the public benefit test. Equally, trade research foundations don't qualify because their benefits are confined to members.

That is not to deny the sponsor and/or charity the right to patent the patentable outcome of such research, and a reasonable delay in publication to accommodate this (perhaps six months to a year) would probably not invalidate the charitable nature of the research.

Heritage charities would include those established for the preservation of historic land and buildings but would also cover preserving particular traditions provided the benefit to the public can be shown. The Architectural Heritage Fund (see appendix 1) has produced a model constitutional document.

For sources of further guidance see 5.15.

5.7   Charitable category (g) – the advancement of amateur sport

Prior to the 2006 Act, only a limited range of adult sports organisations could register as charitable: those that fell within the Recreational Charities Act 1958 or, post-2002, those registered under the 'fourth head' as a charity set up to promote community participation in healthy recreation. (An alternative since 2002 has been to set up as a community amateur sports club (CASC) – not a charity but entitled to similar tax reliefs.)

The 2006 Act changes matters by taking away many, but not all, of the barriers to sports charities. They still have to be 'amateur' and there is a specific definition of 'sport' in the Act – 'sports or games which promote health by involving physical or mental skill or exertion'. This would, for example, include chess but it is not clear whether it will cover sports previously denied charitable status, such as billiards and ballooning.

Organisations now able to take advantage of charitable status will include single sport clubs that select on the basis of aptitude or fitness, and sports clubs with non-playing social members. Also, charitable status should now be an option for sports' governing bodies involved solely with the amateur game, and organisations that arrange amateur leagues and competitions.

Registration as a charity under the Recreational Charities Act 1958 still remains an option and may be useful for organisations providing general recreational facilities.

An updated version of the Charity Commission publication RR11: *Charitable Status and Sport* is expected sometime in 2008. For sources of further guidance see 5.15.

5.8   Charitable category (h) – the advancement of human rights, conflict resolution or reconciliation, or the promotion of religious or racial harmony or equality and diversity

Directly upholding basic human rights – such as those embodied in the European Convention on Human Rights after World War II – was only fairly recently clarified as charitable. The passage here of the Human Rights Act 1998 was the straw that finally broke the Commission's excessively cautious approach. Before that, registrations were possible, but by circuitous legal routes – such as educating the public in human rights and research in relation to the same. How we lawyers toiled!

The Act confirms the recent (and welcome) developments in Charity Commission policy, but be aware that promotion of peace (at least within England and Wales) remains outside the scope even of this category. Even now (and rightly), a human rights charity cannot have as an express constitutional purpose the changing of the law, here or elsewhere (which is why Amnesty failed in its famous court battle for charitable status). Furthermore, even a registered human rights charity will need to watch its step with regard to its means of campaigning and the limited types of political activities charities can carry out – see chapter 13 for more details.

For sources of further guidance see 5.15.

5.9 Charitable category (i) – the advancement of environmental protection or improvement

Previously, charities of this kind were registered either as educational charities or under the 'fourth head'. Now, provided an objective case can be made to show that the particular resources, land or habitat to be conserved is worthy of conservation, there is no need to wait until it is endangered. It covers anything from specific animals to wildlife in general, areas of natural beauty and the environment generally. This category also includes a mixed bag of zoos and organisations promoting recycling and sustainable development/biodiversity.

Promotion of the environment, sustainability and promotion of climate change are also now accepted as being within this section. The Commission is responsive to new ideas in this dynamic area provided there is a reasonable demonstration of cause and effect, backed up by research.

For sources of further guidance see 5.15.

5.10 Charitable category (j) – the relief of those in need by reason of youth, age, ill-health, disability, financial hardship or other disadvantage

Charities falling within this category used to be registered under the umbrella of 'relief of poverty', with poverty interpreted broadly to cover those regarded as 'poor' in non-monetary ways. This new category specifically covers charities where relief is given by the provision of accommodation or care.

Housing associations

New housing associations could register under this category. Most housing associations with selection criteria focused on the relief of need are charitable and many register as industrial and provident societies (see 6.7). The National Housing Federation (NHF, see appendix 1) provides model rules for a charitable housing association (latest version is 2005 Model Rules). The NHF describes this model as 'suitable for associations formed by social, religious and similar groups for the provision of accommodation for persons in necessitous circumstances, e.g. the relief of poverty, general family housing among the lower income groups, as well as the elderly and the disabled'. Housing associations are separately subject to strong regulation by the Housing Corporation.

For sources of further guidance see 5.15.

5.11 Charitable category (k) – the advancement of animal welfare

Previously, animal charities were established under the head of 'other purposes beneficial to the community' on the grounds that their objects could be said to benefit the public, for instance by sensitising public morality through prevention of cruelty to animals. Now such reasoning will no longer be necessary, as the advancement of animal welfare on its own is sufficient to demonstrate a charitable purpose.

For sources of further guidance see 5.15.

5.12 Charitable category (l) – the promotion of the efficiency of the armed forces of the Crown or of the efficiency of the police, fire and rescue services or ambulance services

The inclusion of this might at first sight seem at odds with the charitable purpose of the promotion of conflict resolution. However, the efficiency of the armed forces has long been an accepted charitable purpose and the same is the case for charities promoting the efficiency of the police and other emergency services. Charities falling within this category also include those providing memorials, maintaining regimental chapels or maintaining a military museum, and provision of an emergency air or sea rescue service. In this last area, there is some overlap with category (d), above.

For sources of further guidance see 5.15.

5.13 Charitable category (m) – any other purposes accepted as charitable on the day the Act came into force or which are analogous to or within the spirit of the purposes listed in the Act

This category is intended to include any existing charitable purpose not included in the 12 specific categories. Examples of charities falling within this category include those for the relief of unemployment (this overlaps with category (a) – see 5.1.), the rehabilitation of offenders and the prevention of crime, the promotion of moral or spiritual welfare or improvement of the community, the defence of the country (such as trusts for national or local defence), and the provision and repair of public amenities (such as libraries, public toilets, bridges, highways and ports).

Evolution of new charitable purposes

Equally important is the role of this category to allow for the further evolution of what is regarded as charitable. New charitable purposes can be recognised if they are analogous to, or within the spirit of, the other 12 specific purposes. In the past, a similar catch-all category provided fertile ground (if not without lengthy dialogue with the Commission) for the expansion of recognised charitable purposes in line with developments in social attitudes. The retention of this catch-all category will allow for the continuing evolution of the meaning of charity.

If you think your organisation falls within this category, search the Charity Commission's website (see appendix 1) and look at the objects clauses of similar or analogous charities, to see how they have been worded.

5.14 Objects covering more than one charitable category

It is often advantageous when drawing up objects to refer to more than one of the 13 charitable categories. This provides flexibility in a changing world. Although the Commission may press for quite specific objects, the determining factor should be the best interests of the charity, bearing in mind, particularly, that it is very difficult to extend charitable objects at a future date. You should, therefore, ensure you are satisfied that the objects are wide enough to cover all foreseeable future development.

5.15   Further information

The Charity Commission has already produced a wealth of guidance about how it will interpret the 13 categories and this should be read together with the general guidance and the sub-sector guidance on public benefit. The Commission's website is the best starting point (www.charity commission.gov.uk). You can look in particular for the following guidance and publications:

- Commentary on the descriptions of charitable purposes in the Charities Act 2006
- Charities and public benefit (and the sub-sector guidance)
- CC4:   *Charities for the relief of financial hardship*
- CC6:   *The relief of sickness*
- RR1(a): *Recognising new charitable purposes*
- RR2:   *Promotion of urban and rural regeneration*
- RR3:   *Charities for the relief of unemployment*
- RR4:   *The Recreational Charities Act 1958*
- RR5:   *The promotion of community capacity building*
- RR9:   *Preservation and conservation*
- RR10:   *Museums and art galleries*
- RR11:   *Charitable status and sport*
- RR12:   *The promotion of human rights*

5.16   Some modern types of charity

This section describes current law and practice as they affect some modern types of charity.

Self-help

Perhaps the most common form of mutual self-help groups are those established by and for disabled people and those established for healthcare. Alcoholics Anonymous is one of the best-known groups of this type. Other examples are charities established by and for people affected by HIV/AIDS and those caring voluntarily for housebound people. If such groups were set up and run by a closed group of people merely for their own benefit they would not be charitable however worthy their aims.

But they do qualify if their activities, as well as their objects, are genuinely for the public benefit and available to all those within the area of benefit.

The essential charitable attribute of open membership means that exclusion or expulsion from membership may only be for good cause (such as refusal or failure to pay a reasonable membership subscription, or conduct seriously damaging to the charitable work).

For other types of self-help organisations such as local conservation groups, 'in need' housing associations and neighbourhood and community associations, there are model charitable constitutions that provide for local control. They are often available from a relevant umbrella body.

Where self-help is involved express constitutional authority is necessary if some trustees are to benefit (see 9.5–9.9).

Disaster appeals

Following confusion as to the nature of the Penlee Lifeboat Disaster Appeal in the 1980s, the Attorney General issued a helpful statement on disaster appeals.

Specialist advice should be taken immediately because the wording of the first appeal (often over the airwaves) may set the seal on all that follows. (If you need pointing in the right direction, the Charities Aid Foundation or National Council for Voluntary Organisations can help – see appendix 1.)

You have three choices – a charitable appeal, a non-charitable appeal, or a choice for givers by setting up both. If you choose the last option you must also make clear which of the two appeals contributions will go to if the giver fails to specify which the donation is intended to benefit (as will often be the case).

The decision as to the type of appeal will depend on whether you want its trustees to have unfettered discretion on how to spend the money (in which case you should plump for the non-charitable fund) or a discretion limited by the law of charity.

The main consideration may be that if public sympathy is overwhelming and the appeal attracts a mass response, it could mean that passing all the donations to the injured and bereaved would give them more than charity law would consider to be 'appropriate to their needs'. This would have been the case with the main Penlee Fund, had it been a charitable fund.

That in turn would have meant that a large slice of the donations would have had to be kept back from the bereaved and applied for related charitable purposes.

Wording for a charitable appeal might be:

> To set up a charitable fund to relieve distress caused by the accident/ disaster at Charityville on [date]. The aim is to use funds to relieve those who may be in need of help (whether now or in the future) as a result of this tragedy in accordance with charity law. Any surplus after their needs have been met will be used for charitable purposes designed to help those who suffer in similar tragedies and/or to benefit charities with related purposes and/or to benefit the local community.

These conditions will give reassurance to those donors who feel that too much help is no help at all. But those who feel that no sum is too much for the injured or bereaved will want their gifts to go to a non-charitable fund.

Only donations to the charitable appeal out of taxable income save tax (see 11.1). As regards gifts out of capital, those to a charity are free from inheritance tax without limit, but exempt non-charitable annual gifts are limited to £3,000 (see 11.1).

This means that interest earned on the accumulated fund is liable to tax if it is a non-charitable appeal. However, given efficient distribution, this may be a relatively minor matter.

Relief of distress

Although the Charity Commission no longer likes words such as 'distress' to describe charitable purposes, because it considers they are difficult to define, organisations such as the Samaritans and the London Gay and Lesbian Switchboard, which relieve 'suffering and distress', are, properly, charitable.

Advice giving

If you can clearly show that the advice to be given is educational and/or will be instrumental in relieving a charitable purpose (such as poverty) it should be possible to obtain registration. Some law centres, for example, have registered with objects that include 'to relieve poverty by providing free legal advice and assistance to persons resident in Charityville ... '.

The Charity Commission can become anxious where such advice services are also available to those who are well off. This should not prevent registration, however, where the advice to be given is in furtherance of a plainly charitable purpose – e.g. advice about public environmental law (but see 5.2, 'Business education'; and training for the relief of unemployment, 5.1 and 5.13). Nor will a charity be prevented from freely educating the public generally, whatever the subject.

Support charities – 'Friends' and the like

Schools, colleges, places of worship, local museums and heritage sites – themselves all charities – increasingly spawn separate support charities (often called 'Friends of' this or that) to aid their work, mainly by fundraising and volunteering. That is not strictly necessary, because in most cases such Friends can be established under the wing of the charity supported (i.e. within the existing constitutional framework).

However, the internal dynamics may favour separate organisations. Despite extra administrative expense, it can motivate supporters to put more effort behind what they will feel to be 'their show'. It will also give the governing body of the Friends real independence and discretion as to the timing and application of the funds raised.

Ethnic organisations/race relations

Groups set up to relieve poverty, advance education or pursue other charitable purposes among people of a particular ethnic group, for example Muslims, Irish or West Indians, can usually obtain charitable status provided those benefits are not restricted by reference to colour or race as such. An acceptable phrase to describe, for example, second generation immigrants is 'people of West Indian ethnic origin'. Many such community-type charities are being established these days.

Promotion of good race relations is charitable if you define the objectives in such terms as 'the advancement of education in good citizenship'.

6 Legal formats and constitutional requirements

6.1 Introduction

Those forming a charity are well-advised to work out, sooner rather than later, exactly what they are seeking to achieve, and by what means. Every charity must have a set of rules (a 'constitution') by which its legal status is clear and by which its internal arrangements and procedures are governed. In putting together your constitution you should seek to:

- define the scope of the objects/purposes/aims/ends of the would-be charity clearly, and as widely as possible, and also the means of achieving them (the 'powers');
- build in balanced, practical arrangements for the charity's governance, likely to foster the good and equitable conduct of its affairs, including means of appointment (and removal) of the trustees and of members (if any), plus arrangements for committees, any branches, possibly an advisory council or the like, membership fees, changing the constitution and dissolution.

6.2 Choices of legal format

The major options are:

- unincorporated organisations;
- corporate organisations.

Unincorporated organisations

There are two alternatives:

- trusts;
- unincorporated associations, societies or clubs.

Corporate organisations

The choices here are:

- limited companies;
- friendly societies;
- industrial and provident societies;
- Royal Charter bodies;
- charitable incorporated organisations (expected to be available sometime during the course of 2009).

6.3   Unincorporated and corporate charities compared

The trust

Charitable trusts – a unique flowering of English legal culture – have been used since time immemorial to facilitate and safeguard gifts. Such a trust arises where a donor agrees with the trustees (i.e. those the donor entrusts) to put into their hands money or other property (the trust property) to be used exclusively for charitable objects specified by the donor.

The trust relationship, simple in concept, can also be simple to create – word of mouth being technically sufficient. However, the Charity Commission, not surprisingly, requires written evidence of the existence and nature of the trust so that it may determine whether it is charitable.

The trust is usually ideal for simple or narrow purpose charities, small-scale charities and charities not looking for formal constitutional participation by volunteers or members. It is also often the best format for fund-giving charities, however large, where questions of trustees' potential personal liability will not be a real issue.

Quick and often relatively cheap to set up and run, the trust was long regarded as the traditional format for charities.

The drawback of the trust is that its trustees enjoy no limited liability, so if they overextend or underinsure their charity they can end up being personally liable (see chapter 9). This is a major issue and must be properly considered.

The unincorporated association, society or club

These are membership organisations where the relationship between members is determined by contract in the form of the constitution. A committee is usually elected to run the organisation on behalf of the members (committee members are, as such, also its trustees). They have direct accountability to members and can only make them personally liable if the constitution so allows or the members so agree. The committee is in the same position of personal liability as trustees of a trust.

The corporate organisation

The major legal difference between corporate and unincorporated organisations is that a corporate organisation is more than the sum of its parts. It has a legal identity independent of its members. Thus, while it is only able to act through human agents (usually called its directors), the corporation has its own rights and duties, and holds its own property rather than through trustees.

A limited company, for example, is only born when the Registrar of Companies (at Companies House – see appendix 1) issues its 'promoters' (the people who apply for incorporation) with a certificate of incorporation (which includes its registered name and number).

A corporate organisation provides significant protection for its members and its trustees/directors against personal liability, as compared with trusts and unincorporated organisations.

Liability – the unincorporated charity

The principal disadvantage of the charity established as a trust or unincorporated association, society or club is usually perceived to be the unlimited personal liability to which members of its governing body (whatever it may be called) could be individually exposed. They will usually be personally liable under contracts entered into on behalf of the charity; if it is sued, their names will appear on the court documents, and it is they who will, if all else fails, have to pay any damages. They are then jointly as well as individually (or 'severally') liable, so that a rich trustee could end up carrying the load for his or her poorer colleagues. In that event he or she will have a right of equal contribution from each of them, but that may not be collectible.

Although, of course, trustees will normally be entitled to be reimbursed out of the charity's assets, this will be of no consolation if the cupboard is bare. They will then have to stump up out of their personal assets if no more funds can be raised to cover the deficit and the creditors are legally pursuing payment.

Common examples of liabilities that trustees of unincorporated charities often take on (whether or not they realise it) are service, hire purchase or rental payments and obligations under a tenancy (including repairs). There is also the possibility of the charity being sued for negligence or unfair dismissal, or for liabilities to its pension fund, or having its financial planning wrecked because of fraud. If it is uninsured or underinsured, the trustees could end up personally liable for the aftermath if there are insufficient charity assets to meet those and other liabilities, and no prospect of raising extra funds.

However, these risks can be – indeed often are – exaggerated. Insurance is available for most things and specialist trustee indemnity insurance policies are available covering many (but not all) risks of personal liability for trustees – see 9.5. Also bear in mind that the trustees of a charity – whether unincorporated or in corporate form – are supposed to be circumspect about financial risks and prudent in budgeting. That is to say, obligations generally should only be incurred as and when the resources to meet them are either in hand or are more or less assured. The law requires prudence.

Further, trustees will not be personally liable for obligations incurred where it is a term of the contract that they are only liable to the extent of the charity's assets. It is therefore good practice to try to negotiate such a limitation in relation to all long-term or potentially heavy contractual commitments (such as in leases).

Liability – the company

The limited company format was developed in the 19th century to allow an unconnected group of people to invest capital for a common, specific commercial purpose, but so as to safeguard their other assets.

Having said that, few trustees will be content to walk away from liabilities to innocent third parties they have incurred on behalf of their corporate charity, even if they legally can.

The 'wrongful trading' provisions of the Insolvency Act 1986 will anyhow strip trustees/directors of the protection of limited liability if they knew or ought to have known that there was no reasonable prospect of the company avoiding insolvent liquidation. Rightly, the law does not allow directors to be irresponsible at creditors' expense. However, this is a difficult test to apply and professional advice should be taken well before that position is reached. It would be a very rare case for creditors to pursue trustees under the wrongful trading law.

Quite apart from that, the limited liability status of a charity will not protect its directors against personal liability if they permit it to operate *ultra vires*

– beyond its charitable scope (or objects) – or are otherwise in breach of their duties (such as paying themselves without constitutional authority). This is because the directors of a corporate charity are also its charity law trustees, and subject to both the Companies Acts and charity law.

Trustee indemnity insurance is also an important consideration for trustees of a corporate charity (see 9.5).

Day-to-day formalities compared

The informality and flexibility of the unincorporated body may be appropriate where the charity is for a limited, or local, purpose or where it is well blessed with reserves, or is a grant-giving charity and hence generally indifferent to liability issues. In all other cases operating on a corporate basis is likely to be more appropriate.

Not to have to comply with company law requirements for holding meetings, filing resolutions, lodging annual returns and so on was once considered a benefit, especially for unpaid volunteers. However, most administrative requirements of company law now have direct charity law equivalents and basic administration is a matter to which those involved with any charity should apply themselves.

More significantly, non-incorporation can leave trustees exposed. If serious disagreements break out, one is normally left relatively unsupported in terms of constitutional provisions to head off or resolve them. At such times the mass of detailed company law provisions that automatically apply can prevent the substantive disagreement being complicated by a host of procedural ones. However, non-compliance with company law provisions can give rise to their own problems.

The new legal form, the charitable incorporated organisation (CIO) (see 6.5), has been created in a bid to offer charities the advantages of limited liability status without involving the complexities of company law.

For the membership charity the corporate form is likely to be the right one. It provides the necessary regulation, control and certainty, plus a worked-out constitutional relationship between the trustees/directors and the members.

Similarly, for any charity with more than one or two employees, with obligations in relation to premises or which is involved in service provision, the corporate form is likely to be more appropriate. It means the charity itself is the employer, tenant or service provider and this removes the complications of individual trustees having direct personal responsibility and potential personal liability for such matters.

It may be useful to look around and see how other successful charities of your type organise themselves.

Constitutional changes compared

Provided that the trust deed or other unincorporated governing document was drafted to allow changes in its terms, the speed and ease of effecting them can be an advantage compared with the obligatory procedures for companies. Changing a company's Memorandum and Articles (its constitution) involves formal notices, prescribed time periods, a precisely worded special resolution and subsequent filing obligations. The rules for CIOs are likely to be similar.

Summary of benefits of trust/company/CIO

Benefits of trust	Benefits of company	Benefits of charitable incorporated organisation
• Quick and cheap to form. • Easy and 'forgiving' to run. • No dual public filing requirements. • Fewer mandatory constitutional demands than for companies. • No Company Registrar equivalent. • Usually easier to change constitution (trust deed).	• Provides limited liability protection for trustees/directors and members. • Provides a panoply of arrangements under company law controlling many/most aspects of running of the company. • In particular, provides a framework detailing trustees'/directors' and members' roles. • Can hold property, employ staff and deliver services in its own name.	• Provides limited liability protection for trustees and members • Can hold property, employ staff and deliver services in its own name • Only reports to one regulator, the Charity Commission But note that, because this is a new entity, it is not yet tried and tested.

6.4   Company formation

Limited by shares or guarantee?

There are two main types of limited company. The norm in the field of commercial activity is the company limited by shares. This is almost always an unsuitable format for a charity to adopt. The other type of company, appropriate for a charity, is the company limited by guarantee.

Constitutional arrangements

Companies are governed by the Companies Acts 1985 to 2006. Company constitutions consist of a Memorandum (containing objects and powers) and Articles of Association (internal rules and regulations) – though the 2006 Companies Act contemplates a single constitutional document in the future.

The Companies Acts provide a ready-made, comprehensive framework which, tailored to the circumstances of the particular charity, will usually cope with the day-to-day pressures and strains which are the lot of any dynamic, participatory charity. Regulations under the Companies Acts provide a company limited by guarantee with model Articles of Association. These include detailed provisions for holding members' and directors' meetings, voting rights, and a myriad of other matters.

Within certain limits, about which a lawyer will advise, the promoters can add to or subtract from the Companies Acts model Articles as they think fit. Most modern charitable companies have specifically drafted Articles, which should be much simpler and easier to read than traditional drafting.

Normally anyone can be a member if the directors admit them to membership within the constitution. Powers of removal/expulsion should also be provided (subject to good cause and the principles of natural justice). The nature of charity is to favour open membership.

However, there are many possible arrangements vis-à-vis new members and election or appointment of directors. Getting them right for your charity's needs can be vital.

There are also occasions when the membership may comprise various classes, which will need very careful consideration and drafting.

There is much talk these days of good governance, too much of it 'production-line', so beware.

The Companies Act 2006 makes some changes to the way that companies are run and formed. It is being implemented in stages and is expected to be completely in force by the end of 2009.

Directors/trustees v members

Companies have a two-tier power structure – members and directors/trustees. Although the directors hold day-to-day management power, the right of removing them must (by the Companies Acts) ultimately rest with the members of the company. Appointment, ironically, can wholly or partly rest elsewhere (even with an outside person or body).

By contrast, there is often no check on the longevity in office of trustees of a trust other than their consciences and any limitations in the trust deed. Thus, if they regularly fail to use their powers effectively there may be no practical means of unseating them.

The two tiers of the company format, designed to provide checks and balances, can be simplified by prescribing that the two groups – members and trustees/directors – shall be the same.

Usually neither the Charity Commission nor the courts will interfere on questions about the quality of the trustees' performance, but only in relation to its propriety according to the terms of the constitution and general charity law. (Trustees should, however, be aware of the extent of their responsibilities and potential liabilities – see chapters 8 and 9.)

All charities must have at least two trustees and the Charity Commission normally expects to see at least three. There is no maximum prescribed by law. Traditionally charitable trusts choose to have an odd number of trustees to avoid deadlock, without having to give the chair a casting vote. The constitution should clearly specify the circumstances in which trustees can be elected or appointed and removed, by what procedure and by whom.

Incorporation

Incorporation involves submitting to Companies House the original Memorandum and Articles signed by the first members; Companies Form 10 containing signed consents of the first directors/trustees and company secretary to act; a statutory declaration of compliance; and, if desired, confirmation that, as a charity, the company is entitled not to have the word 'limited' in its name. The fee is £20 for the standard service, which takes eight to ten days, or £50 for the 24-hour service. There is some scope for the papers to be filed electronically, usually through advisers.

6.5   Charitable incorporated organisations

A new legal form, designed specifically for charities, is due to become available sometime in 2009, thanks to the Charities Act 2006. The charitable incorporated organisation, or CIO, will be a limited liability vehicle that will need to be registered with the Charity Commission, but not with Companies House. This will avoid the burden of dual regulation, which has always been a disadvantage of the charitable company option (albeit a relatively minor one with the increasing regulation of all charities).

A CIO must have a constitution, and will have a two-tier structure, like a company, of members and trustees, although they can (as with a company) be the same people. The constitution of a CIO must address a number of issues, including how members and trustees are appointed. CIOs must disclose their CIO status on certain public documents, including cheques and business letters.

CIOs will be formed by sending a copy of the proposed constitution to the Charity Commission. There should be no fee. Once registered in the register of charities, the CIO can open its doors for business. There are special procedures allowing existing charities to convert to CIO status.

The Charities Act 2006 sets out a broad framework for CIOs; further details will be found in regulations which, at the time of writing, had not yet been published and had been considerably delayed.

The government has heralded the CIO as a more flexible alternative to the charitable company. Time will tell whether it lives up to its expectations. It is certainly a positive move that charities will be able to use a vehicle that has been specifically created with the sector in mind, should they wish to. But there are some concerns that CIOs may be almost as hampered by red tape as companies limited by guarantee. The government has also suggested that once the CIO has been available for five years, it will consider whether the other forms of incorporation should remain available to charities. This would be a real blow: the CIO is a useful alternative to the existing legal forms but should not be regarded as a replacement for those that work well.

6.6 Friendly societies

Friendly societies were an invention of the 19th century when a massive number of these self-help voluntary associations were set up to stave off the terrors of sickness, severe poverty and misfortune. It is a traditional structure for groups concerned with mutual relief of hardship. They may be charitable if the beneficiary class is confined to those in need. Today they are of fast declining popularity.

A charitable friendly society is currently exempt from registration with the Charity Commission but must register with the Financial Services Authority (see appendix 1). Larger friendly societies are, however, due to fall within the Charity Commission's net before too long (see 7.4). Friendly societies registered under the Friendly Societies Act 1992 have corporate status.

6.7 Industrial and provident societies

Characteristics

The Financial Services Authority (FSA) also has the statutory job of overseeing industrial and provident societies (IPSs) under the 1965 Act governing them. An IPS is a society for carrying on an industry, business or trade, either as a 'bona fide cooperative' i.e. for the benefit of its members, or as a 'community benefit society'. Only an IPS within the second category may be charitable.

An IPS is currently exempt from registration with the Charity Commission, although this is due to change for some larger IPSs (see 7.4). If you plan to set one up, it is wise to send a draft set of rules to the Charity Division of HM Revenue and Customs (see appendix 1) to obtain its guidance on whether it would accept the IPS as charitable for tax purposes. This is the nearest you can come to gaining advance recognition.

Applicants, other than housing associations, may find it difficult to satisfy the two sets of requirements – those for being charitable and those for being an IPS. To benefit the community, the IPS's rules must prohibit the distribution of its assets among members. Control should be vested in the members equally and only moderate interest can be paid on share or loan capital. Other requirements are set out in the first schedule to the 1965 Act.

While it is recognised that the IPS format is useful, it is underused by charities. This is partly because the IPS regime is largely dealt with by the 1965 Act, which is in dire need of modernisation. At the time of writing, HM Treasury is considering how the IPS legal framework can be brought up-to-date.

IPS and company compared

The rules and formalities of the IPS are less rigid, complex and onerous than those for companies. This no doubt relates to the fact that an IPS was not (as a company was), designed primarily as a vehicle for profit-generation.

An IPS can convert into a limited company, and will be able to convert to a CIO. A company can likewise convert to an IPS. Unless it consists of two or more registered societies, an IPS requires at least three members.

If an IPS registers using model rules submitted through a 'promoting society' such as the National Housing Federation, it can be quite quick and cheap to register and you are unlikely to need a solicitor. The FSA has a special fee for applicants using approved model rules of £40, which rises according to the number of required adaptations to the model. Registration with a bespoke draft will take longer and the maximum fee is £950. The FSA also charges annual fees, which vary according to the society's financial position.

6.8   Royal Charter body

This ancient format, which gives limited liability and corporate status to those bodies which enjoy it (not all of them charities), is in the gift of the Privy Council representing the Crown and is now very rarely bestowed. If it is, the constitution will be bespoke and subject to approval by the Privy Council Office, as will any variations. It is a stately process.

6.9   Your constitution

General

The constitution (whether trust deed, unincorporated association rules, Memorandum and Articles of Association or other governing instrument) is to a charity as bricks are to a house. If wrongly put together, it can seriously blight the charity for ever more. Unless you are following a model that really does fit you should get advice from someone experienced in drawing up (drafting) constitutions.

Objects (or purposes, aims, ends)

By far the most important clause of any constitution is that which defines what the organisation exists to do i.e. its objects. For an organisation to be charitable the objects must be drafted with technical proficiency to ensure that they are, in law, exclusively charitable (see chapter 4). An otherwise proper application for charitable status can be badly set back by an objects clause which, through inexpert drafting, does not fit the bill. Above all, resist the temptation to draw up the objects as a ringing declaration of your ideals. The Charity Commission will insist they be redrafted, and your public appeal will anyhow need a different style and content from the legal document.

In drafting the objects, it is vital to define them so that if circumstances change, or the organisation evolves away from original expectations, its new activities will still be within its bounds.

It is helpful for trustees to understand that it is entirely up to them to decide how the charity operates within its objects. They can ignore 90% of their scope and concentrate all activities within the other 10%. No one can attack them on legal grounds.

Powers

The constitution should clearly define the powers (or means) by which the objects can be promoted. A 'power' is a discretion and need not be exercised. As with the objects, it usually pays to give your trustees/directors maximum room for action, i.e. the widest powers.

It is worth mentioning that if they are given the power so to do, the trustees/directors can themselves make internal rules or 'standing orders' for the administration of the charity. That may, for example, be for meetings, or about use of charity property. Such day-to-day arrangements may not be suitable for inclusion in the constitution itself, and can be brought in and phased out simply by trustees'/directors' resolutions.

The trustees/directors need constitutional authority to delegate the exercise of their powers; this is an important issue (see 8.8).

Other powers it is usually wise to include are those of lending and borrowing, employing, insuring (including standard provisions for trustees' indemnity insurance), acquiring and occupying property, altering the constitution, trading, setting up related companies and charities and winding up the charity. Several of these topics are enlarged upon elsewhere.

Trustees/directors

It is the trustees of the trust or CIO, the directors of a company, and the committee of an unincorporated association (all of whom are charity trustees) who have ultimate policy and executive power in a charity. The scope of their authority should be clearly defined, especially if there are other, lesser sources of power (such as advisory councils, branches or regions). It is essential that you describe how and when trustees can be removed and new appointments made. Think about the wisdom (or otherwise) for your charity of a prescribed retirement procedure for trustees, maximum terms in office, renewed terms, rights of co-option, nomination of trustees by other bodies and so on.

All these issues and more relating to trustees and their liability are covered in detail in chapter 8.

Members

As explained earlier, most trusts do not have members separate from their trustees. All companies, CIOs and other unincorporated associations do (though the two groups can be made co-extensive if appropriate). One must clearly define the members' rights and duties, how new members can be admitted and existing ones removed. It is also essential to work out precisely the constitutional relationship between members on the one hand and trustees/directors on the other.

Altering the constitution

The Companies Acts compulsorily provide that a company may amend its constitution by special resolution (i.e. one passed by a 75% majority of those voting at a members' meeting or, where the resolution is in writing, by 75% of the members eligible to vote). CIOs will be able to change their constitution by a resolution passed by a 75% majority of those voting at a members' meeting, or by unanimous written resolution. The constitution of a trust or unincorporated association should provide a power allowing the constitution to be amended, but if there is no such power the Charities Act 1993 (as amended by the 2006 Charities Act) now contains various statutory powers for the trustees to make constitutional changes, which may help.

However, the objects clause and any other constitutional provisions with a direct bearing on the application of charitable funds, such as in respect of winding up or the non-remuneration of trustees, cannot be changed without the consent of the Charity Commission. In the case of a charitable company or CIO this is stipulated by the Charities Act 1993; in the case of unincorporated charities it is the general law as regards remuneration of trustees and (unless the constitution clearly so allows) alteration of the charitable objects.

All changes to the constitutions of registered charities must be filed with the Charity Commission. In the case of CIOs, the changes are not effective until the Commission has registered them. Charitable companies must also register changes with Companies House.

Elections

If you are to elect any of the trustees/directors or officers, then the mechanics must be spelt out to avoid confusion and constitutional malfunction. For example, do they rotate on fixed terms (e.g. one third retire every year) or stay put until they resign or are voted out? Are there provisions for direct nomination by interested parties?

Investment

It is important to define, and to define widely, trustees' investment powers. The Trustee Act 2000 may, for unincorporated charities, be satisfactory (see 8.9).

Dissolution and surplus assets

It is essential that a dissolution clause states what should be done with any surplus left on dissolution, after all the charity's obligations have been paid off. The law requires that it should go to another charity, or for charitable purposes, otherwise monies that have been donated to the charity could find their way to non-charitable causes.

Often the arrangement is that any surplus goes to another charity operating in a similar field chosen by the majority of the trustees, or the members. Sometimes that charity is actually named in the dissolution clause. Alternatively, discretion can be left to the trustees. For example:

> The assets of the charity (if any) after payment of all proper debts and liabilities shall not be paid or distributed amongst the members but shall be given to such other charitable organisation or organisations with objects similar to those of the charity as the members for the time being shall decide or in default of any such decision within a month of the resolution to dissolve as shall be decided by the trustees (all such decisions to be by simple majority).

If the charity is likely to be registered with the Office of the Scottish Charity Regulator, or with an equivalent body in Northern Ireland, the dissolution clause may need to make it clear that the ultimate recipients on a winding up are regarded as charitable in those jurisdictions as well as in England and Wales (see 4.5).

Discontinuance without dissolution

If there is no dissolution clause in the constitution of a charity and no amendment clause enabling one to be inserted, or if the means by which such an insertion can be made or a dissolution clause implemented cannot be triggered (perhaps because unanimity is needed and one trustee is holding out), there is an alternative. This will be for all the assets of the charity to be given away within its objects (having met or made full provision for its liabilities, actual or contingent).

Merger

It is increasingly common for charities in the same field with compatible objects to join forces. Rather than dissolving both such charities and creating and registering a new one to which all the net assets of the wound-up charities are transferred, it often makes sense to select one of them as the continuing vehicle and transfer assets from the other charity into it.

That will only be done when the charities have reached comprehensive agreement on the future basis of their merged activities. This will cover such issues as staff, debts and other liabilities, constitutional changes to the continuing vehicle, its governing body, broad future policy, name and whether there are any special trusts or endowments for which special provision needs to be made.

A constitutional power should be included allowing for this possible future development, to avoid otherwise unnecessary engagement with the Charity Commission.

A new development under the Charities Act 2006 is the establishment of a register of mergers kept by the Charity Commission. Where mergers are registered, not only will there be a public record of the arrangement, but gifts to the 'discontinued' charity which take effect after the merger, such as legacies, will automatically be treated as gifts to the continuing 'merged' body. An alternative way of dealing with the prospect of future legacies is nominal continuance of the 'discontinued' charity, which was sometimes the only option in the past. There are also new mechanisms under the 2006 Act designed to facilitate the merger process.

Conversion to a company or CIO

It is not uncommon for charities first established as trusts or unincorporated associations to decide to reconstitute as a company. This involves the registration of a new corporate charity with its own charity registration number, a legal transfer of the existing trust's operations – such as assets, liabilities and staff – to the company and provisions to protect the trustees of the trust from the possibility of future personal liability. The assets will have to be ringfenced for use for their original objects. The cost of this operation will be similar to the costs of the original establishment, so if a charity is, at the outset, considering future development that may warrant incorporation, it may be preferable to establish itself as a corporate organisation from the beginning. Again, a constitutional power should cover this possible development.

A similar process will be necessary if an unincorporated charity wishes to become a CIO. A new charity – the CIO – will need to be set up, and the assets and liabilities of the unincorporated charity transferred to it. If the constitution of the unincorporated charity does not contain a power to transfer property in this way, there are some powers in the Charities Act 2006 which may help.

6.10   Charity Commission models

For applicants for charitable status with no special constitutional needs, there are model charitable constitutions provided by the Charity Commission free of charge – one each for trusts, companies and unincorporated associations. It is likely that similar models will be available for CIOs. These may be read alongside a selection of Commission guidance documents (see appendix 2), which give a good picture of what is required.

The applicant will still have to draft the appropriate charitable objects, which are the heart and soul of the constitution. Where the charity is a conventional one, this should be reasonably straightforward (especially as the Commission will be more inclined to assist if its model has been used).

However, a model is a drafting aid, not a passport to registration. There is no more pernicious self-injury than to skimp the real constitutional needs of the charity to ease the path to registration.

7 Applying for charitable registration

7.1 Registration requirements

Before you can register as a charity you will need to have established your organisation, in whatever form, with a charitable constitution (see chapter 6). Except in the case of charitable incorporated organisations (see 6.5) the Charity Commission (which covers charities in England and Wales) will now only pre-consider a draft constitution in special cases.

To register a charity in England and Wales the Commission will require:

- a copy of the governing document;
- a completed standard application form and a standard declaration form signed by each of the trustees (available from the Commission as part of its application pack);
- evidence that the charity's gross annual income is over £5,000, which can include a letter pledging funding.

An English or Welsh charity with a gross annual income of over £5,000 is obliged to register with the Commission (see 7.2) unless it is an exempt or excepted charity, although the rules regarding exempt and excepted charities are due to change from late 2008 (see 7.4 and 7.5).

For details of registering a charity in Scotland or Northern Ireland see 7.12 and 7.13.

7.2 HM Revenue and Customs

In order to take advantage of the tax reliefs available to charities (see chapter 12), charities will need to contact HM Revenue and Customs (HMRC). HMRC generally accepts that organisations registered with the Charity Commission or the Office of the Scottish Charity Regulator (see 7.12) are entitled to the tax breaks due to charities under the tax rules. However HMRC can and will refuse tax relief where a charity has not in fact applied taxable receipts for charitable purposes (see 12.2).

7.3   Small charities

Charities with an annual income of £5,000 or less are not required to register with the Charity Commission. Although they may apply to register on a voluntary basis, at the time of writing the Commission's policy is to accept such applications in exceptional circumstances only. These include cases where there is specific evidence that significant grant funding rests on the organisation being registered with the Commission.

Charities with income below the threshold that are not registered with the Commission should seek direct registration with HMRC. Charitable companies and unincorporated associations are obliged to be registered with HMRC regardless of income, and it is good practice for small charitable trusts to do so.

Note that the rules about voluntary registration of small charities are due to change, but not until 2009 at the earliest. When the relevant sections of the Charities Act 2006 come into force, charities with income below the £5,000 threshold will have a right to register if they wish to.

Registered charities with income of £10,000 or less do not need to publicise their registered status and are subject to a relatively benign reporting regime (see chapter 10). Unregistered charities are generally free from the Commission's reporting requirements, although they do have to maintain proper records and accounts and the Commission has some powers to request copies of accounts and reports (see chapter 10).

7.4   Exempt charities

Some charities are exempt from many of the administrative provisions of the Charities Act 1993. They are, for the most part, listed in section 3 of or schedule 2 to the Charities Act 1993 and, at the time of writing, include foundation and voluntary schools, universities, museums, housing associations and other charitable industrial and provident societies. Exemption means they cannot register with the Commission and they do not have to produce annual accounts, reports or returns to the Commission unless requested to do so. The basis for this exemption is that they are supervised by another regulator, although at present none of these other regulators specifically monitor performance with reference to charity law.

The Charities Act 2006 changes the rules on exempt charities, although the new regime is not due to be implemented until 2009. Some classes of charity will lose their exempt status, notably industrial and provident societies and friendly societies (unless they are registered social landlords registered with the Housing Corporation) and foundation and voluntary schools. But these charities will only be required to register with the Commission once their income is over £100,000. The government may decide, over time, to reduce this threshold.

Where charities remain exempt, their existing regulator will have a new responsibility to ensure that they comply with charity law. The Charity Commission will also have wider powers to intervene in the activities of exempt charities.

7.5   Excepted charities

There is a separate category of charities which, although not exempt, are excepted by order or regulation from the need to register. These include some religious charities and the Scouts and Guides. The basis for their exception is that they are registered with large umbrella or support groups.

The Charities Act 2006 also makes some changes to the rules for excepted charities, due to come into force in late 2008. Excepted charities with annual income of over £100,000 will have to register with the Charity Commission. Again, the government has power to reduce this threshold over time in order to oblige more excepted charities to register.

7.6   The application form

The Charity Commission's application form includes a series of questions aimed at eliciting your plans, for example by reference to intended beneficiaries, proposed activities and fundraising. Your answers require care, and sometimes advice. The critical section is the description of the proposed activities and a clear statement of how these activities will promote the charitable objects and deliver public benefit. Where, as is often the case, the promoters of the charity are genuinely uncertain about the programme its trustees will adopt (often because financial resources are uncertain without registered status or because the governing body has not had the chance to allow ideas to develop and mature), this should be plainly stated. The worst mistake is to set out over-detailed or grandiose plans which, in the event, the charity does not or cannot carry through.

The form contains a specific section for charities working with children or vulnerable people, designed to ensure that appropriate policies are in place and that appropriate Criminal Records Bureau checks have been carried out on the trustees.

7.7   The Charity Commission's 'gateway' policy

The Charity Commission has a legal obligation, subject to the minimum registration requirements (see 7.2), to register an organisation established with exclusively charitable objects. However, the Commission investigates, sometimes in depth, the proposed charity's organisation, business planning, financial planning and proposed activities and now, in all cases, whether the organisation fulfils the public benefit requirement (see 4.4). This is described as the 'gateway' policy.

A reasonable policy designed to help can become unfair and a hindrance if unreasonably applied or handled by inexperienced staff. Sometimes a meeting is the best way to sort out problems. Occasionally it may be necessary to lodge an appeal or complaint at the appropriate level within the Commission. The best course is a careful and precise initial letter accompanying the application form that anticipates any concerns the Commission might have. Expert advice is particularly helpful in this respect.

So, be thorough and anticipatory in the preparation of your application to register, and provide as detailed a list of proposed activities as you can, cross-referred to the objects, and a practical indication of anticipated means of raising funds.

However, all you can legally be asked to show is good sense and reasonable preparation for your charity's future, not that everything is planned to the last detail. Many charities start only with aspirations, and they are entitled to do so.

7.8   When to apply

It tends to be easier to register a newly established organisation as a charity than one which is already up and running. Therefore, if you think that it may be to your advantage to register earlier than you need to, go ahead. It will avoid, for example, problems with inaccurate publicity about your activities, which can give the Charity Commission the wrong idea.

If you need to start operations before registration (for example, to take on premises or employ a key person), make sure that the constitution allows any amendment to be made for the purpose of achieving charitable status.

Some organisations start out unclear about whether the charity route is best for them. This may be covered by deliberately drafting a non-charitable object alongside the charitable ones, which can then be removed if necessary, if and when the decision is made to pursue registration.

Note, however, that charitable status is recognised, not conferred, by registration. Thus, once you establish with exclusively charitable objects you are a charity and so entitled to the charity tax reliefs from that time, not from subsequent registration. You should persist if these are initially denied.

7.9   Difficulties in registration

Be patient, polite and constructive in your dealings with the Charity Commission. Be well briefed and flexible. If you are convinced you have a good case, persist. If an application is likely to prove difficult, don't wait until you have been rebuffed to get good advice. Second attempts are always more difficult.

Even well prepared and apparently straightforward applications can meet with a disappointing initial response from the Charity Commission and different case officers can have different approaches.

Sometimes a meeting with the person dealing with your case will help. Sometimes it is better simply to persevere in correspondence, producing fuller facts and more persuasive legal backing to support your application. The Charity Commission will sometimes suggest how you should change the wording of your draft constitution .You may have to drop or alter some of your proposed objects or powers, but do take expert advice if you are unhappy about or unsure of the impact of the Commission's suggestions. It is ill-advised to 'buy' consent by restricting your objects in a way that could have serious consequences.

If you feel you are being unreasonably cross-questioned, or are asked inappropriate or irrelevant questions (perhaps because of lack of understanding of the issues), this should, sooner rather than later, prompt a request for a meeting or (as appropriate) an official appeal or complaint.

7.10   Appeals and complaints

If, after corresponding with the Charity Commission you think its refusal to register your organisation is legally wrong, you can ask for the case to be formally reviewed. At the time of writing, the review involves a two-stage process, with the second stage being conducted by the Charity Commission's Board. The Commission is currently considering a proposal to streamline the process so that only one stage is involved, with no guaranteed involvement by the Commission's Board.

The reviews are currently free and this is unlikely to change.

If your appeal is rejected by the Commission, currently the last recourse is an appeal to the High Court with scope (in theory) for an appeal to the Court of Appeal and finally (with consent) to the House of Lords. 'In theory' because few, if any, can contemplate the high cost of such proceedings, for which legal aid is not available. If you lose, you may also be liable for the other side's costs.

However, the Charities Act 2006 has introduced a new avenue of appeal against many of the Commission's decisions, by establishing an independent Charity Tribunal (up and running since March 2008). The Tribunal has been designed as a quick and cheap way for charities to challenge the Commission's decisions, although only time will tell whether it will live up to these expectations.

A formal complaint about the Commission (as opposed to a formal request for a review of a decision) may be made to the Commission itself, with scope to complain further to the Commission's Independent Complaints Reviewer if not satisfied with the outcome.

7.11   Fees

The Charity Commission, the Office of the Scottish Charity Regulator (see 7.12) and HM Revenue and Customs do not charge registration fees, but you will have separate establishment fees if you set up as a company, an industrial and provident society or a friendly society (see chapter 6).

7.12   Scotland

Charities established in Scotland now need to register with the Office of the Scottish Charity Regulator (OSCR). OSCR will require a copy of the governing document, a completed application form and trustee declaration form, and a document giving details of the organisation's activities or intended activities.

Charities already registered with the Charity Commission, or which are applying to register with the Commission, may also need to register with

OSCR if they are contemplating certain activities in Scotland. The requirement to register in both jurisdictions will depend on whether the charity occupies any land or premises in Scotland or carries out activities in an office, shop or similar premises in Scotland. It is a good idea for charities that think they may be in this position to take legal advice, as registering in both jurisdictions is a bureaucratic process, and may affect what the charity's constitution can say.

7.13   Northern Ireland

Northern Ireland has conducted a review of its charity law and at the time of writing wholesale reform is expected in 2008. This is likely to include the establishment of a Charity Commission for Northern Ireland (CCNI), which will operate along the same lines as the Charity Commission in England and Wales and OSCR in Scotland. Charities already registered with the Charity Commission in England and Wales which also operate in Northern Ireland may also need to register with CCNI.

In the meantime, an organisation based in Northern Ireland wanting charitable status should draw up its draft governing instrument and submit it for clearance to the Charity Division of HM Revenue and Customs (see appendix 1).

The Department of Social Development in Belfast (see appendix 1) can advise charities and prospective charities.

8 Charity trustees and running a charity

8.1 Charity trustees

The term 'trustee' can be confusing. All charities must have charity trustees whatever name they are known by. In the Charities Act 1993 charity trustees are defined as 'the persons having the general control and management of the administration of the charity'. The constitution of a charitable trust (a trust deed) invariably refers to its trustees as such, and the constitution of a charitable incorporated organisation (see 6.5) will do the same. In a charitable company, company directors (usually so called) are also by law its charity trustees. In an unincorporated charitable association, club or society, members of its management committee (by whatever name called) fulfil that role and are its charity trustees. In this chapter the word 'trustee' covers all these roles.

Choosing the right trustees for a charity is vital. It can also be a bit baffling. Should you invite friends, or eminent names, or local worthies? What qualities or abilities will the trustees need? Can they be paid? What responsibilities are they taking on? How much can be and should be expected of them?

8.2 Trustees' responsibilities

In a nutshell, the trustees of a charity have full responsibility for, and control of, what the charity does and how it uses its funds and assets. Their overriding duty is to ensure that the charity's objects are effectively promoted in accordance with its constitution. This general duty may be expressed more specifically as follows:

- to be responsible for the proper administration of the charity;
- to act reasonably and prudently in all matters relating to it;
- to safeguard and put to good use its assets;
- to act collectively to make the best of the charity;
- to avoid any conflict of interest;
- to 'have regard to' the Charity Commission's guidance on public benefit.

The Charity Commission issues the booklet *The Essential Trustee: what you need to know* (www.charity-commission.gov.uk). Also see chapter 9 for information on trustees' liability.

8.3 Choosing trustees

The trustees should ideally be a team of contrasting and balanced virtues appropriate to the nature and level of activity planned for the charity. Bear in mind that the trustees collectively have the final say and can override the staff, volunteers, committees, branches and all. It is far more important that they are likely to prove committed and capable than that they are eminent. Obviously, and in all cases, they need to be absolutely trustworthy.

A relevant balance of skills, age, gender and experience is desirable; so too may be an ethnic and religious spread. Overall, a body of trustees that is able, wise, balanced and harmonious is the aim. And a bit of fun does not go amiss. Trustees are, after all, volunteers.

The Charity Commission is not usually directly concerned with the personal identity of proposed trustees, unless they have particular concerns (for example, relating to potential conflict of interest).

To be established in the UK (for tax and registration purposes) an unincorporated charity must generally have a majority of its trustees resident in the UK or major assets and an office here. The corporate charity achieves that by incorporating in the UK, although the Charity Commission may express a preference for a UK majority on a corporate board, requiring specific explanation as to why this is not appropriate in a particular case (for example where the charity is intended to operate as an international organisation).

8.4   Patrons

There are benefits from having well-known people publicly associated with your charity. But since they are, by definition, likely to have many other calls on their time, one can sometimes get the best of both worlds by engaging these celebrities as 'patrons' (or whatever) rather than trustees. 'Patron' is normally a purely honorary title, which does not give its bearer formal power or responsibility. Preferably, though, it will mean some level of active support.

8.5   Paying trustees and worker trustees

It has always been a fundamental presumption of English common law that trustees of a charity should not make any direct or indirect profit out of their office, nor be placed in a position where their duties as trustees might conflict with their personal interests. Any exceptions to this rule must be either contained in the constitution or allowed under the Charities Act 2006 if they are to be effective. Barring some fairly standard exceptions, the Charity Commission will generally refuse to register an applicant whose constitution allows benefits over and above some limited and generally accepted categories.

Payment for goods and services

One of the most widely accepted exceptions is to allow trustees or their firms to be paid for goods or services which they provide to a charity, other than for acting as a trustee or under a contract of employment. This means that if, say, one of the trustees is a builder or a fundraiser they can carry out building or fundraising work for the charity, and be paid for doing so. Historically, this was only allowed if the constitution contained a specific power along these lines. It was usual for the power to require that the trustee concerned should not be involved in discussions about awarding him or her the work, and there may be a restriction on the number of trustees who can receive a benefit of this nature at any one time.

From March 2008, the Charities Act 2006 introduced a new power for trustees to be paid for services provided to, or on behalf of, the charity, provided certain conditions are met. The conditions include ensuring that the payment is reasonable, the trustees being satisfied that it is in the best interests of the charity for the services to be provided by the trustee, having a written agreement in place, and limiting the number of trustees who are paid to a minority at any one time. Trustees are disqualified from taking part in any decisions relating to the agreement. The power will apply regardless of what the constitution says, except where the constitution contains a restriction on paying trustees, which may well be the case. This could be a trap for the unwary but other provisions of the Charities Act 2006 should facilitate removing any such restrictions so the statutory power can be relied upon. The power does not allow payment for simply acting as a trustee or actual employment by the charity, as opposed to providing specific services.

Paid or employed trustees

Where the trustees wish to receive some payment for actually acting as a trustee, or it is proposed that a trustee should be a paid member of staff, this must be provided for in the constitution or specific Charity Commission approval sought. The Commission will only accept that trustees should receive payment in these circumstances if it can be satisfied (and it takes some convincing) that the particular charity will get major benefit if the request is granted or suffer significant damage if it is denied. Here are some such possibilities:

- A charity being established by the effort and the reputation of one person which, for it to be a success, will need him or her to work full time as well as being a trustee.
- A large, very active charity needs one paid, or part-paid, executive trustee in order to hold its operations together and provide the necessary leadership.
- A beneficiary or community-driven charity needs some staff on the governing committee to exemplify its essentially self-help nature (e.g. citizens advice bureaux have employees on their committees).

The Commission will require that such trustees must always be a minority and be absent when the committee considers matters in which they have a personal interest.

8.6   Trustee expenses and benefits

Whether or not one seeks to have remunerated trustees, it is normal and acceptable to provide in the constitution for payment of out-of-pocket expenses incurred in connection with acting as trustees.

It is also normal and permissible for there to be express provision for payment of reasonable interest on monies lent to the charity, or rent for property let to it.

8.7   Conflict of interest

It is an iron rule of charity that trustees must seek to avoid a situation in which their charitable duty and personal interests conflict.

This is at its most acute where, for example, a trustee is selling something (including services) to, or buying something from, the charity of which he or she is a trustee. This can lead to severe legal consequences if proper precautions are not taken to avoid the conflict by insulating the relevant trustee from the transaction. This is no less true of corporate charities: the fierce provisions of the Companies Acts apply to charitable companies, and the Charities Act 2006 will prevent the trustees of a charitable incorporated organisation from benefiting from transactions unless appropriate disclosures have been made. In some cases, such as contracts involving land, specific Charity Commission consent may be needed even if the constitution appears to authorise the transaction.

This handbook is not the place for a full explanation of this subject, and legal advice should be taken when direct or indirect conflict (for example involving a spouse or partner) may be looming. Steps which can be taken to minimise the scope for a conflict include maintaining a list of each trustee's external interests, asking as a matter of routine at the start of meetings whether there are any conflicts to declare, and ensuring that trustees are excluded from discussions in which they may have an interest which conflicts with that of the charity.

8.8   Delegation of trustees' powers

It is a basic rule that trustees cannot delegate their decision-making powers unless the charity's constitution expressly allows. It is vital that it does. This will, for example, enable the charity to devolve certain day-to-day decisions to an executive committee, or to set up committees for special purposes or projects.

A clear and comprehensive general delegation power is desirable in almost every case (even if only to provide flexibility for an unknown future).

Under the Trustee Act 2000 unincorporated charities are permitted to delegate functions to an investment manager. However, companies need to provide for specific delegation to an investment manager to carry out delegated functions. The Trustee Act 2000 provides a useful model for the clause a company needs.

Trustees can only delegate on the basis that they can withdraw, or alter, the terms of that authorisation at any time. Make sure in all cases that it is absolutely clear what powers or role you are delegating, and to whom. It is also important to require any committee to report regularly to the trustees and to inform them promptly of their decisions. Above all, it is essential to be clear about whether the committee can commit the funds of the charity, for what purposes and up to what amount.

The operation of bank accounts raises a direct tension between trustee accountability and practicality. Arrangements should be crystal clear and carefully observed, especially where there is delegation. It usually makes sense for the governing body to be able to instruct the bank to accept the signatures of whomever it considers appropriate, including signatories who are not on the governing body. The Charity Commission will often seek to insist on two trustee signatories, and will be correct in warning that for trustees to leave cheque signing to others can mean undue risk. In busy charities a trusted senior executive could be entrusted with cheques up to a modest limit, with two signatories – including at least one trustee – for higher value cheques, and two trustee signatories for major expenditures.

8.9 Trustees' powers

General

Subject to the objects clause and applicable legal requirements, the golden rule is normally to give trustees (and therefore their charity) the widest powers and discretions relating to, for example, how it is managed, how it may fundraise and apply its assets and how to invest any surplus assets.

Investment powers

The Trustee Act 2000 changed the law significantly for unincorporated charities. Unless the constitution of the charity otherwise provides, the Act allows trustees to invest in anything as long as they take account of their general obligation to take due care and have regard to the standard criteria when exercising their powers. Charitable companies, if set up with narrow powers, may exercise their statutory powers of constitutional amendment to broaden them.

In all cases, trustees must exercise reasonable care and skill when deciding how to invest and when reviewing existing investments. This means acting with the prudence of someone investing the funds of another person for whom they feel morally responsible. This obligation will be heavier in the case of a trustee who professes to have certain expertise, or who might be expected to have such expertise, because of his or her work. Trustees must have regard to:

- the need to balance income, capital growth and security;
- the suitability of the investments (which may include the need to take account of ethical concerns, mentioned below);
- the need to have a reasonable spread of investments;
- the need to avoid undue risk (they should never gamble).

Trustees must obtain and consider proper advice, unless they reasonably believe that outside advice is unnecessary, for example because there are expert trustees, or the sum to be invested is relatively small.

There is also always the possibility of investing in a charity common investment fund. (Such funds are authorised by the Charity Commission as appropriate investment vehicles for charities and have unrestricted investment powers.) This is often a good idea for smaller charities. For example, three common investment funds are available from the Charities Aid Foundation (see appendix 1).

Ethical investment

A question charity trustees should consider is whether, by law, they must give paramount consideration to purely financial considerations when investing, or whether non-financial factors may have a determining influence?

The view until relatively recently was that ethical considerations are only admissible if there is no financial cost, in terms of income, capital growth or security. This had much to do with a narrow reading of the judgement in the miners' union fund case, Cowan *v* Scargill.

The position is now reflected by the Charity Commission's following statement:

> *Whilst the normal duty of charity trustees in exercising their investment powers is to provide the greatest financial benefits, financial return is not in all cases the sole consideration. Charity trustees should not invest in companies pursuing activities which are directly contrary to the purposes or trusts of their charity. It would, for*

example, be entirely appropriate for the trustees of cancer relief charities to decline to invest in tobacco companies.

This seems blatantly obvious, but over-cautious trustees still abound. At root, everything that trustees decide on behalf of their charity must seek to be consistent with its charitable purposes. Where these are broad and general, the ethical considerations are likely to be less clear. Where, however, the purposes are particular, then certain investments will not only be ill advised, they may even be unlawful, whatever the financial benefits. These dilemmas may be acute for religious charities.

Trustees should also take account of the impact of sensitive investments on the charity's donors, would-be donors, staff and volunteers, and on its standing with its beneficiaries. It is also relevant to have regard to the reputation of the charity at large, particularly where its influence is important to delivery of its charitable effort.

All this was made clear in a landmark case of Harries (The Bishop of Oxford) *v* Church Commissioners and is discussed in the current Commission guidance on the subject.

It is often difficult to form a sensible judgement about the application of ethical criteria. A real danger is that some trustees may allow personal views to get in the way of objective evaluation.

However, in the changing world investment climate, more and more charities are concerned to invest in a manner ethically supportive of their objects. Investment funds are being established which observe ethical criteria in a manner (they claim) consistent with high performance. The UK Social Investment Forum (UKSIF) and Ethical Investment Research Services (EIRIS) are in the vanguard of this movement (see appendix 1)

8.10   Appointing and replacing trustees

Such matters need particular thought in every case. Note what other charities you respect do.

The usual system for a charitable trust is that the trustees hold office until they retire or are removed. In a trust set up by an individual, one can provide that the power of appointment is exercisable by the founder (though the Charity Commission may question a personal right to remove trustees). Where nothing is provided, the Trustee Act 1925 gives power of appointment to the continuing trustees.

In the case of corporate charities, it is common to provide for automatic retirement by rotation of trustees/directors, typically after three years in office.

Other possibilities include nomination by relevant outside bodies, ex-officio appointments (e.g. the local mayor will automatically be a trustee for his or her term of office) and election by different categories of member.

Whatever the system, your constitution should specify who has the power to appoint or elect and who has the power to remove trustees. If it is a corporate charity these powers invariably reside in the members, who can include donors, volunteers, employees and, indeed, beneficiaries. Other arrangements are possible. For example, some community charities elect their committees at open meetings, where any local person can attend and vote.

Note, however, that if the charity is a limited company nothing can deprive its members of the right to remove any or all of its trustees/directors at any time under the Companies Acts.

The Charity Commission has extensive power to discharge trustees and officers of a charity in cases of misconduct or mismanagement. This may follow an official inquiry, or a crisis where the charity cannot be properly protected without that intervention. Any person interested in a charity's affairs can make representation to the Charity Commission in relation to such matters.

Under section 72 of the Charities Act 1993 someone who has been convicted of a serious crime, is bankrupt, makes an arrangement with creditors to avoid bankruptcy, is disqualified as a company director, or is mentally incapable, will also be automatically disqualified from acting as a charity trustee.

The Charity Commission has to keep a register of those thus disbarred. There are criminal sanctions for breach of the prohibitions.

8.11   Charity accounts

There is a legal obligation to keep proper accounts consistent with the needs of the charity and it is important to institute an appropriate bookkeeping system from day one. Small charities can use very simple systems but if you fail to set one up early enough or fail to operate it assiduously you will store up time-consuming problems and may not be able to keep financial control and effective management. Furthermore, without evidence of proper financial systems you may find it difficult to obtain funding.

Proper records will, of course, form the basis of the annual audit or independent examination of your charity's accounts (see 10.4).

In preparing for formal accounts the Statement of Recommended Practice (SORP) for Charity Accounts will be applicable to most charities. The Charity Commission has produced various publications to assist in complying with SORP (see www.charity-commission.gov.uk).

9 Liability of trustees/directors

9.1 Personal liability with no relief – for wrongful behaviour

Charity trustees (note the meaning – see 8.1) who act dishonestly, or with reckless or wilful negligence, either in relation to their own duties, or in allowing their charity to act ultra vires (outside the scope of its constitution) will be personally liable for any loss, without limit, to whoever incurs the loss and/or to the charity itself. There is little hope of relief from such liability (see 9.2). The trustees will not be covered by any indemnity insurance in any of these cases (see 9.5).

9.2 Personal liability with possible relief – for negligent behaviour

Where a charity incurs loss through inadvertent breach of trust or other negligence by its trustees, short of the culpability inherent in the cases referred to above, the trustees can be called to personal account by the High Court or the Charity Commission and made personally liable to the charity. However, that will be rare. Even in such a case the Court or Commission has a discretion to – and often will – relieve trustees of personal liability where there is no bad faith. That will not protect trustees against losses incurred by outsiders ('third parties'), though that should be covered by general and/or trustee indemnity insurance (but see 9.5).

If charity trustees are worried about whether a proposed course of action on behalf of the charity is reasonably justifiable, they should seek advice from a solicitor or the Charity Commission, though the Commission's advice is likely to be conservative and can be a long time coming.

However, formal sanction, or advice, given under the Charities Acts by the Commission in knowledge of the full facts and acted upon may give protection to charity trustees against an action for breach of trust (but not third party claims).

9.3   Unincorporated charities

Since an unincorporated charity has no legal identity beyond that of its current trustees, any liability of the charity will attach to those who were the trustees at the time the liability was incurred. A properly managed system of appointments and retirements will pass on such responsibility, in relation to legitimate liability, to the current trustees. There is, though, exposure to individual personal liability if the charity has insufficient funds to meet its liabilities.

The committee of an unincorporated membership association can only reimburse itself from the membership if the members agree or if the constitution clearly gives it the right.

9.4   Limited liability

As explained in 6.3, the trustee of a corporate charity is at a significant advantage if the charity becomes insolvent. However, a charitable company's trustees/directors can be held personally liable to creditors for wrongful trading (see 6.3) and there are a number of other rare and particular situations, for example in relation to health and safety, where a company director can, as such, be exposed to personal liability.

9.5   Trustee indemnity insurance

A charity can take out and pay for an indemnity policy to cover its trustees' risks of personal liability, except those mentioned under 9.1. Such a power may appear in the constitution, but in early 2007 the Charities Act 2006 introduced a power for charities to take out and pay for trustee indemnity insurance, subject to certain safeguards, even if there is no constitutional power.

Such insurance is now seen by many prospective trustees to be an important protection against the much over-hyped personal risks of trusteeship but, for the vast majority of trustees, there is in reality little threat of being found liable for such liabilities. The more meaningful benefits are comfort and cover for legal costs if an issue does reach a point where defensive action is required.

10 Regulatory requirements

10.1 Introduction

Charity trustees must, of course, operate within their charity's constitution and observe both charity law and the general law (for example vis-à-vis employment, land and contracts). There may also be separate regulations arising from a charity's particular legal status (e.g. limited company) or its activities (e.g. housing association or credit union).

The 1992, 1993 and 2006 Charities Acts and many subsidiary regulations, together with the accounting Statement of Recommended Practice (SORP), have established a highly regulated environment for charities.

The Charity Commission has generated further policies, which acquire quasi regulatory significance. There are also other regulators to keep in mind, such as Companies House, the Financial Services Authority, the Housing Corporation, the Information Commissioner (in relation to data protection), local authorities, and HM Revenue and Customs.

It is beyond the scope of this handbook to map this jungle completely, but it does address some key issues. The Charity Commission's index of guidance publications is another useful reference point (see www.charity-commission.gov.uk).

10.2 Publicity requirements

Every registered charity with income over £10,000 must state on charity letters and other documents its name and the fact of registration, which in practice generally means stating its charity registration number. This threshold may be increased to £25,000 later in 2008.

Charitable companies and industrial and provident societies can benefit from exemptions from the requirement to have the word 'limited' in their names. They must instead indicate their status by including it on all official correspondence and documents, by stating (respectively) 'a company limited by guarantee', or 'an industrial and provident society'.

Similar rules will apply to charitable incorporated organisations (CIOs). If a CIO's name does not include 'CIO' or 'charitable incorporated organisation', the fact that it is a CIO will need to be stated on official correspondence and documents.

Limited companies' stationery should also state the place of registration, (i.e. England and Wales, Scotland or Northern Ireland), its registered company number and its registered office address. It must name either all its trustees/directors, or none.

Non-compliance with these provisions is an offence (though enforcement is all but unheard of).

10.3   The Charities Acts 1992, 1993 and 2006

At the time of writing, the main statutory provisions regulating charities are contained in three Acts – the 1992, 1993 and 2006 Charities Acts. This means that navigating the rules can be difficult, particularly since not all provisions of the 2006 Act are currently in force. They will be coming into force in stages over three to four years. Ideally, these three Acts should be consolidated into one new Charities Act. This is said to be in the pipeline. In the meantime the patchwork of charity legislation looks like this:

The Charities Act 1992

Part II of this Act sets out regulatory provisions controlling fundraising deals between charities and professional fundraisers/commercial participators (see 11.1) imposing requirements to make fundraising statements in certain situations.

The Charities Act 1993

This Act contains most of the statutory provisions applying to charities, many of which are referred to elsewhere in this handbook. The Act is amended substantially by the Charities Act 2006, although this is not yet fully in force. The outline regulatory structure of the 1993 Act, as it will look once the whole of the 2006 Act is in force, is as follows:

- Sections 2A–2D (part IA) deal with the Charity Tribunal.
- Sections 3–7 (part II) set out basic registration and disclosure requirements (see 10.2).
- Sections 8–20A provide the Charity Commission with extensive powers to protect charity assets and to inquire into, and intervene in, the operation of charities for that purpose.

- Sections 26–31A provide support powers to the Commission, including powers to authorise dealings with charity property and ex gratia payments and to give authoritative advice.
- Sections 36–40 (part V) set out important self-policing arrangements for selling, leasing and mortgaging charity land which would otherwise require Commission consent.
- Sections 41–49A (part VI) set out the regime for accounts, reports and returns, including audits, independent examination and rights of public inspection (see 10.4).
- Sections 63–69 (part VIII) set out specific provisions applying charity regulation to charitable companies.
- Sections 69A–69Q (part VIIIA) deal with charitable incorporated organisations.
- Sections 72–73 set out provisions relating to the disqualification of individuals from acting as charity trustees.
- Sections 73A–73F cover remuneration of trustees, trustee indemnity insurance and trustee liability.
- Sections 74–75B give unincorporated charities various powers to deal with their property, including permanent endowment.
- Sections 75C–75F deal with charity mergers.
- Sections 76–79 authorise local authorities to maintain an index of local charities and encourage co-operation between them.
- Sections 81–83 provide statutory administrative provisions, such as allowing two or more trustees to execute documents under section 82.

The Charities Act 2006

Much of the 2006 Act simply amends the 1993 Act, but a few provisions are 'stand alone':

- Sections 1–5 (part 1) deal with the meaning of charity and the public benefit requirement (see chapters 4 and 5).
- Sections 45–66 introduce a new regime for public charitable collections – expected to be in force some time after 2010 (see 11.1).

10.4   Annual accounts, audits, reports and returns

(See the table at the end of this section for a summary of these provisions.)

Accounting records

All charities must keep proper accounting records for at least six years. This means sufficient accounting entries and records from which formal accounts can be adequately prepared and which must be made available to the public on request.

Audits, independent examinations and small charity provisions for unincorporated charities

Every unincorporated charity must carry out a full annual audit of accounts if:

- gross annual income exceeds £500,000; or
- gross annual income exceeds £100,000 *and* aggregate assets exceed £2.8 million.

Where gross annual income and expenditure is between £100,000 and £500,000 (and aggregate assets are £2.8 million or less), an independent examination of statutory accounts by an independent qualified accountant is sufficient; if annual gross income exceeds £250,000, the independent examiner must have an appropriate accountancy qualification.

Where gross income and expenditure is between £10,000 and £100,000, it is sufficient to have an independent examination of statutory accounts by an independent person who is reasonably believed by the trustees to have the requisite ability and practical experience.

Currently, all such accounts must be submitted to the Commission and are generally available to public scrutiny.

For all charities with gross annual income not exceeding £10,000 simple receipts and payments accounts may be prepared and must be made available to the Commission and the public on request.

Be aware that some of these thresholds may change in late 2008 – the Commission has consulted on increasing the audit threshold to £1 million and the threshold for independent examination to £25,000.

Company law accounting regime for charitable companies

The requirements for charitable companies under the Companies Acts are:

- a full audit of accounts where there is a gross annual income of over £500,000 (or a balance sheet total over £2.8 million) in the relevant or preceding financial years;
- a reporting accountant's audit exemption report where aggregate assets are £2.8 million or less and the gross annual income is between £90,000 and £500,000;
- exemption from Companies Act audit requirements where there is gross annual income of less than £90,000.

At the time of going to press it is expected that from 1 April 2008, charitable companies below the audit threshold will be brought within the charities accounting regime.

All charitable companies must submit their annual accounts to Companies House within 10 months of the end of the financial year to which they apply. Charitable companies with gross income exceeding £10,000 must also file their accounts with the Charity Commission.

Annual reports

Every registered charity must make an annual report, which will be open to public inspection. Charitable companies must also submit an annual report, under company law, to Companies House. Current practice is for a more extensive charity law report to suffice for both. Annual reports are, in practice, invariably submitted with the accounts.

From 2008, trustees will have a new duty to include in the annual report a statement detailing how the charity's aims have been carried out for the public benefit. Charities below the unincorporated charity audit threshold (see above) need only provide a brief summary of activities. Larger charities above the audit threshold must provide a fuller explanation.

Annual returns

All registered charities with gross income over £10,000 must submit an updating annual return to the Commission – the form increases in complexity with the charity's level of gross income. A separate form is required to update registered company law information (returnable to Companies House).

Group accounts

From 1 April 2008 there will be a new requirement for unincorporated charities with subsidiaries under their control to prepare group accounts, subject to a minimum threshold.

10.5   Default in submissions to the Charity Commission and Companies House

Default in the basic filing obligations set out above is an offence by the responsible trustees, unless they can show that they took 'all reasonable steps' to secure compliance. The Director of Public Prosecutions has to consent to any prosecution; in practice prosecution is only likely in the most extreme cases. The Charity Commission has a naming and shaming policy and Companies House can levy automatic late filing penalties (which can be, but usually are not, payable personally by directors).

10.6   Accounting Statement of Recommended Practice – SORP

Professionally produced charity accounts must, in practice, also comply with the Charities Statement of Recommended Practice (or SORP). This covers the preparation of accounts and annual reports, and supplements the relevant statutory provisions and regulations. The current version of SORP is SORP 2005, which represents a significant extension of the original SORP, introduced in 2000. It deals with accounting practice for charities producing full accruals accounts, and contains guidance in relation to charitable companies and for the treatment of (among other things) 'subsidiary' undertakings and other connected or associated organisations. SORP will be adapted to accommodate accounting changes under the Charities Act 2006.

Although not statutory, all chartered accountants will be governed by SORP in preparing charity accounts, and should only depart from it for good, formally stated, reasons.

The Commission publishes a range of very useful booklets in relation to the accounting regime applicable to charities (see www.charity-commission.gov.uk).

10.7   Charity Commission literature

Many Charity Commission policy, advice and guidance documents are available free of charge (see www.charity-commission.gov.uk). They are not legally binding, but usually represent good practice and are best given careful regard. There is a legal obligation to 'have regard to' general guidance and sub-sector guidance on public benefit.

10.8   Internal policies and procedures

Some of the Commission guidance relates to policies that charities are increasingly expected to have in place (though in most cases the appropriateness is still a matter for the trustees). For example, SORP requires a statement in the annual accounts about the trustees' risk management policy. Larger charities should also have (or be clear why they do not have) reserve, investment, health and safety, equal opportunities and data protection policies, plus appropriate disciplinary and complaints procedures. There may be other policies appropriate to particular charities (for example child protection) or required as a matter of good administration (for example conflict of interest or staff email use). These are all really applications of the trustees' general duty to act reasonably in their management functions, but familiarity with the issues and relevant Commission guidance is desirable.

10.9   The regulators

The Charity Commission

The Commission has a clear set of objectives, functions and duties, which are now laid down by statute.

The Commission's objectives include:

- increasing public trust and confidence in charities;
- promoting charity trustees' compliance with their legal obligations;
- promoting the effective use of charitable resources; and
- enhancing charities' accountability to donors, beneficiaries and the general public.

Its functions include:

- dealing with questions about charitable status;
- encouraging and facilitating the better administration of charities;
- identifying and investigating misconduct and mismanagement and taking appropriate remedial and protective action; and
- providing information.

These functions combine the roles of friend and police officer of the charity sector.

The Commission has offices in London, Liverpool, Newport and Taunton. General responsibility is divided geographically. On registration charities must provide certain information to the Commission to be held on its register. This is updated annually (see 10.4). The register is open for public inspection and some of the information can be accessed via the Commission's website (see appendix 1). As well as many useful publications (see www.charity-commission.gov.uk), the Commission also provides advice on the telephone and via email.

The Office of the Scottish Charity Regulator (OSCR)

OSCR is the Scottish equivalent of the Charity Commission in England and Wales. English charities operating in Scotland may, depending on their activities, also have to register with OSCR.

Charity Commission of Northern Ireland (CCNI)

CCNI is due to be established some time in 2008. It will register Northern Irish charities and also have some jurisdiction over English and Scottish charities operating in Northern Ireland.

Companies House

Charitable limited companies are subject to company law, including public filing obligations. These, for example, require filing an up to date memorandum and articles of association, the registered office address and details of trustees/directors, company secretaries and charges issued by the company (mortgages over its assets) to be registered at Companies House.

There is a separate obligation to maintain, at the registered office, formal statutory books containing the above information and also the members' register and the minutes of all trustees'/directors' and members' meetings. These are not generally for public inspection, although there are some rights for the public to request access to the members' register.

If you are setting up a charitable company do your homework and obtain timely expert advice as necessary. Companies House (see appendix 1) has a range of free publications available.

The Mutual Societies Division of the Financial Services Authority

Responsibility for both friendly societies and industrial and provident Societies is now undertaken as a department of the overarching financial services regulator, the Financial Services Authority.

The rationale of regulation is essentially the protection of members who have come together and committed themselves, in the case of the charitable community benefit society, to operating for the community benefit.

The Housing Corporation

Housing charities registered with the Housing Corporation (see appendix 1) are registered social landlords and must comply with a raft of other requirements aimed, principally, at ensuring good management and the protection of tenants.

The Information Commissioner

Under the Data Protection Act 1998 an organisation which holds or processes information about individuals must notify the Information Commissioner. This applies to information held on manual records or electronically. Details of the notification procedure can be obtained from the Information Commissioner's Office, via the website or by telephoning (see appendix 1).

Local authorities

Local authorities are important in the financial and practical support of local charities. Many will be closely involved with charities, and may maintain an index of them. They are also responsible for applying the 80 per cent mandatory non-domestic rating relief available to charities and must have a policy in relation to the provision of further discretionary relief, up to 100 per cent (see 12.2). Local authorities are also responsible for issuing street and house to house collection fundraising licences.

HM Revenue and Customs

HM Revenue and Customs (HMRC) oversees the main tax exemptions for charities and the relevant VAT law (see chapter 12). It has a specialist charity unit in Bootle, Merseyside that can give advice (see appendix 1).

In Northern Ireland HMRC is currently the main charity regulator, but this is due to change in 2008 – see above.

Charities Act 1993 accounting/reporting requirements

This table shows the charity and company law accounting/reporting requirements for charities according to charity type. Unregistered and some registered charities may also be subject to other accounting/reporting regimes. Section numbers refer to the Charities Act 1993.

Key to charity types

1 Registered unincorporated: gross annual income over £500,000
2 Registered unincorporated: gross annual income £100,000 to £500,000
3 Registered unincorporated: gross annual income £10,000 to £100,000
4 Registered unincorporated: gross annual income not exceeding £10,000
5 Company: aggregate assets over £2.8 million or gross annual income over £500,000
6 Company: gross annual income between £90,000 and £500,000 (and aggregate assets of £2.8 million or less)
7 Company: gross annual income between £10,000 and £90,000 (and aggregate assets of £2.8 million or less)
8 Company: gross annual income not exceeding £10,000 (and aggregate assets of £2.8 million or less)
9 Exempt charity
10 Excepted charity (other than small charity)
11 Unregistered small charity (income less than £1,000)

Charity type	Accounting records (s41)	Annual accounts (s42)	Audit/independent examination (s43)	Annual report (s45)	Annual return (s48)	Accounts open to public (s47)
1	Yes	Full accounts	Full audit	Yes	Yes	Yes
2	Yes	Full accounts	Full audit if aggregate assets exceed £2.8 million. Otherwise independent examination; if annual gross income exceeds £250,000 the independent examiner must be a qualified person	Yes	Yes	Yes
3	Yes	Simplified accounts	Independent examination	Yes	Yes	Yes

4	Yes	Simplified accounts	No (unless it is a requirement of the charity's governing document)	Yes, and for all charities other than charitable incorporated organisations, filing with Commission on request only	No	Yes
5	Companies Act	Companies Act	Audit under Companies Act and under s69 Commission may audit	Yes in addition to Companies Act report	Yes in addition to Companies Act return	Yes
6	Companies Act*	Companies Act*	Report by reporting accountant, and s69 applies*	Yes, in addition to Companies Act report	Yes, in addition to Companies Act return	Yes
7	Companies Act*	Companies Act*	No, but s65 applies*	Yes, in addition to Companies Act report	Yes, in addition to Companies Act return	Yes
8	Companies Act*	Companies Act*	No, but s65 applies*	Yes, but filing with Commission on request only	No, but voluntary annual information update	Yes
9	No, s46 applies	No, s46 applies	Not under the 1993 Act, but some other statutory accounting provision or SORP may apply	Not under the 1993 Act, but some other statutory accounting provision or SORP may apply	No	No
10	Yes	Same requirements apply as for a registered charity with the same constitution and income/asset levels – see above	Same requirements apply as for a registered charity with the same constitution and income/asset levels – see above	Or Commission request	No	No
11	Yes	Simplified accounts	No – unless it is a requirement of the charity's constitution	No	No	No

* At the time of going to press it is expected that from 1 April 2008 charitable companies below the audit threshold will be brought within the accounting regime of the Charities Act 1993.

11 Fundraising, social enterprise and trade

11.1 Fundraising

General

Fundraising for most local charities is normally a matter of chance and circumstance. Raffles, bazaars, special events and high street collections have been standbys, but things are changing. The larger charity, with paid staff, long-term projects and contract funding will almost certainly be caught up in more sophisticated ways of raising money.

Fundraising deals

The Charities Act 1992 regulates two types of business partner with which a charity may engage to raise funds.

Professional fundraisers are businesses that raise funds directly for charities in return for payment (e.g. a telephone fundraising company). **Commercial participators** are businesses that promote schemes whereby some of the proceeds will go to charity (e.g. a restaurant scheme dedicating a percentage of the cost of meals to a charity). Each is required to carry out such activities only on the basis of a written agreement with the relevant charity and must include, in all promotions, a statement explaining, in the case of commercial participators, how much of the money raised will actually reach the charity, and in the case of professional fundraisers, how much they are being paid by the charity.

Individuals who are paid or rewarded in other ways for fundraising for a charity (for example, with a place on an overseas event) may also fall within the definition of professional fundraiser and the same conditions will apply.

A cautionary note

Before agreeing a fundraising deal, bear in mind the following.

- It can be tricky, so if in doubt get advice.

- A charity cannot carry on permanent or substantial trade not directly related, or ancillary, to its objects. Structured trading activities to raise funds are almost certainly outside this allowance although there are a few trading exemptions that can prove very useful (see 11.3).
- Deals with commercial sponsors to allow them to use (or exploit) the charity's name, goodwill or logo, or to access the charity's lists of membership or supporters, will be trade if the charity is an active partner (as is likely), although there are special arrangements in relation to charity-branded credit cards.
- Activities referred to above are likely to give rise to tax and VAT issues. Often it is best to structure the arrangements via a trading company owned by the charity, which can gift aid its profits, tax-free, back to the charity (see 12.1).
- The charity should never trade in a way that may jeopardise its reputation and goodwill. Even if it structures part of the deal via its trading company, that risk may still exist, especially if the latter's name incorporates the charity's name.
- You should seek advice on possible mitigation of VAT, which generally bites on charities. HM Revenue & Customs (HMRC) will often permit a sponsor to split payments/fees etc. between taxable, VATable payments and donations direct to the charity. Sometimes it can be arranged so that the charity is treated as a 'financial intermediary' and hence is VAT exempt.

Further regulation of fundraising

Unfortunately there is an increasing array of legal obligations to be aware of when fundraising for charities. The following list is by no means complete but will give you some idea of issues to bear in mind:

- Raffles or lotteries – check their legality under the Gambling Act 2005. The Gambling Commission (see appendix 1) may assist.
- Street collections – permits are usually needed from the relevant local authority or police; there is a prohibition on active solicitation and a need to inform the public if collectors are being paid – the Public Factories and Miscellaneous Provisions Act 1916, further statutory regulations and local by-laws apply. Although the Charities Act 2006 sets out a new regime for public collections, this is not expected to come into force until at least 2010.
- House to house collections – permits are usually needed from the relevant local authority and strict rules apply under the House to House Collection Act 1939 and its regulations. Again, reform is expected but not before 2010.
- Selling donated goods – all donated goods, whether new or second-hand, must comply with safety standards and normal retailing laws. Watch out for loose-eyed teddy bears!
- Providing entertainment – you may need to apply for an entertainment licence, which is a single authorisation to supply alcohol, provide regulated entertainment such as a performance of live music or late night refreshment, or any combination of these activities. For events involving recorded music or other copyrights, licences may also be needed from the Performing Rights Society and Phonographic Performance Ltd.
- Sale of food and drink – entertainment licences (see above) may be needed to sell alcohol, and a myriad of food safety regulations are likely to apply.
- Health and safety – the charity itself and/or volunteers organising an event need to watch out for this branch of legislation.
- Appeals and direct mail campaigns – the British Code of Advertising, Sales Promotions and Direct Marketing and EU-based regulations on distance selling and trading by electronic communication (e-commerce) apply to charity appeals. Charities also need to be mindful of data protection laws.
- Donor participation events (e.g. adventure activities and holidays) – these increasingly popular and diverse methods of fundraising require particular attention in relation to issues such as the incidence of

liability, the application of tax exemptions and VAT, and of specific law, such as travel and health and safety regulations.

Now you know – but don't get depressed. Applied common sense is often all that is needed; plenty of advice is available and, failing all else, officialdom will usually only go for provocative disregard or the maverick.

The Institute of Fundraising (see appendix 1) has a code of practice for fundraisers and provides information on fundraising activity. There are also Charity Commission booklets on the subject (see www.charity-commission.gov.uk) and guidance from HMRC (see www.hmrc.gov.uk). There is also a new organisation, the Fundraising Standards Board (see appendix 1), which has been set up as the sector's self-regulation body.

11.2   Social enterprise – charging for services

A key business planning issue for service providing charities is the extent to which they may charge for their charitable services. This is a burgeoning aspect of charity activity today.

A charity may charge fees for services delivered as part of its charitable activity. For example, in delivering care services to older people, or nursery services to parents, or arts, entertainment or recreational services to the general public. This is called 'primary purpose' trading and should be distinguished from trading for the purpose of raising funds to be applied to charitable purposes.

'Social enterprise' is a relatively new coinage for a much older concept, which has now become a successful progressive movement in its own right. It is, essentially, the promotion of a social purpose through a sustainable business model. Many charities are social enterprises and many more operate, in part, on social enterprise principles, through charging for their charitable services while receiving supplementary sources of income, such as grants, donations and the proceeds of fundraising.

Social enterprise principles are particularly important in relation to the delivery of public services by charities, for example in health, social care and education.

The status of independent schools and private hospitals focused attention, during the debates relating to the 2006 Charities Act, on the particular issue of when charging fees that only part of the population may be expected to afford might not be consistent with charitable operation. The suggestion is that, in order to show requisite 'public benefit', the organisation must demonstrate it provides benefits to a wider group than that able to pay high fees – see chapter 4. Charity trustees must 'have regard to' Charity Commission guidance on public benefit and relevant sub-sector guidance, including that for fee-charging charities.

This is a matter of degree and particular circumstance. The general position is that any fee that is charged must be decided upon in a manner that is consistent with the charitable purpose and delivering public benefit. It must therefore be proportionate to the costs involved in providing the service and, where appropriate, be accompanied by the delivery of wider benefits.

Generally, it is important for charities and organisations with which they deal to appreciate that, in delivering services, the contractual arrangements should be based on the same principles as in any commercial situation. The specification of the service should be clear, the price should be fair and the other terms, including the duration of the contract, should be reasonable.

Misconceptions in relation to the issue of contract price have been corrected by recent emphasis on the need for charities to charge on a 'full cost recovery' basis. This means, simply, ensuring that the price charged is sufficient to cover the costs of providing a service. Such 'costs' include overheads and a reasonable surplus, or profit element, to be applied to organisational development and the maintenance of reasonable reserves as required by any business.

As many contractual arrangements are with public authorities, there has also been a major emphasis on the need for reasonable business planning, which is inconsistent with short-term contracts. It is generally accepted that a service-providing contract should be for at least three years.

Such matters are expressed well in the declared 'principles' of the 'Compact between the public sector and the community and voluntary sector', which is now promoted by the Compact Commissioner (see www.thecompact.org.uk). Being aware of the compact principles will help you to judge your approach to any proposed contract arrangement, although, after more than 10 years of existence, the Compact has not yet had a major direct impact on public sector commissioning practice.

11.3 Charitable trading and taxation

A charity proposing to trade will need to satisfy itself of two things – that it is constitutionally able to do so, and that any 'profit' will not be taxed.

Six main categories of trade

Let us consider six categories of trade by a charity (rather than by its trading company) from those two vantage points, i.e. legality and taxability.

- Category (i) – trading unrelated to the charity's objects to raise funds for it.
- Category (ii) – trading related (i.e. ancillary) to the charity's objects which also raises funds to promote the charitable objects.
- Category (iii) – trading exercised 'in the course of the actual carrying out of a primary purpose of the charity', such as running schools and hospitals.
- Category (iv) – trading 'where the work in connection with the trade is mainly carried out by beneficiaries of the charity' (i.e. beneficiaries who are its employees or outworkers), such as workshops for and involving disabled people.
- Category (v) – trading to sell donated goods via shops run by the charity.
- Category (vi) – trading to sell goods produced by ultimate beneficiaries of the charity as a means of relief of their poverty, such as fairtrade shops.

Note that category (vi) is different from category (iv). In (iv) the 'trade' is manufacturing goods rather than retailing them.

The quoted passages in categories (iii) and (iv) are from s505(1)(e) of the Taxes Act 1988.

Category (i) – unrelated trade

- **Legality:** Strictly such trade is generally unconstitutional (ultra vires), so trustees could be liable for any losses, and that is how they had better look at it. However, if the trade is a moderate and traditional form of fundraising (for example, a fete or two, some raffles, a theatre trip for supporters, a few dances) the trustees could legitimately say that they were acting within their power (implied where not express) to raise money for their charity. The fact that there has been no recent court case on all this tells its own tale. The tax exemptions (below) probably also work for assessing the legality limits.
- **Taxability:** There are three specific exemptions – one by statute (Finance Act 2000); the other two by HMRC concession.

- By statute, provided that a charity's gross annual trading income does not exceed £5,000 or, if it does, does not exceed 25% of the charity's total income (including donations etc.) then, subject to a cap of £50,000, the trading income will be exempt from tax.
- By HMRC concession, trading income will be exempt if it is generated by a fundraising event which:
  - is held primarily to raise funds, and this is made clear to those who attend;
  - is one of 15 or fewer events of that kind being held at separate single locations during the financial year of the charity (disregarding events with gross takings of less than £1,000).
- Finally, there is a specific exemption for certain 'society' and 'small' lotteries run by charities. HMRC (see Appendix 1) provides information on these.

Category (ii) – related trade

- **Legality:** Such trade will usually result from the trustees making best use of their charity's assets (such as universities hiring out accommodation and facilities during holiday time). It could also comprise such things as sale of literature and items indirectly related to the charity's activities or provision of minor refreshment facilities to those attending a charity function. All this is perfectly acceptable legally. Ideally, there should be an express power to enable the trustees to trade in this way, provided such trade does not become dominant.
- **Taxability:** HMRC accepts that tax exemptions for category (iii) (see below) are also usually applicable to ancillary trade. Those available in category (i) might also be available in a borderline case.

Categories (iii) and (iv) – primary purpose trade

- **Legality:** Cast-iron. The fact that the mainstream charitable activity is also trading is irrelevant from this point of view.
- **Taxability:** There are no tax implications – there is specific and complete exemption (Finance Act 1988 s502/3) for these two categories of trade.

Category (v) – sale of donated goods

- **Legality:** As with category (ii) the trustees have a duty not to decline gifts, and also to make best use of them. This is a conversion of gifts of goods into gifts of cash and is inherently permissible.

- **Taxability:** HMRC in effect views the resulting proceeds of sale as a gift of income in lieu of the donated goods, rather than income of a trade and thus there is no tax. Such trade will be within the exemption for charities from business rates (see 12.2).

Category (vi) – trading to promote fairtrade products

- **Legality:** This is directly carrying out the charity's anti-poverty objects.
- **Taxability:** This is a fusion of categories (iii) and (iv) and exempt from tax. Note, however, that this is a recent development, started with registration by the Charity Commission of the Fairtrade Foundation, and now developed a stage further via special Oxfam Fairtrade shops. The conditions to be met in falling within this category are rigorous.

Points to watch out for in all categories

- Tax exemption/concession is only available if the profits are exclusively devoted to the charity's objects.
- If charity shops sell more than a minority of new goods they will be in danger of losing tax and rate exemptions.
- The danger in the last case does not arise with fairtrade goods so long as they all come from poor producers and the charity concerned has relief of poverty objects.
- Much trade is also – and primarily – fundraising. The more it is perceived as the latter, and the more related it is to the charity's objects, the more favourable the legal and taxability prospects (see above).
- Watch out for VAT – just because a trade is legal and exempt from income tax doesn't necessarily mean it is also exempt from VAT.
- Ensure that a wide power to trade is included in the constitution.

11.4   Non-charitable trading – the trading subsidiary

The common method used by a charity to undertake trading which it would not be permitted to carry out by charity law and/or for which it would not be exempt from tax is for a separate limited company to be established for or by the charity. It will usually be wholly owned by the charity.

Such a company is not directly subject to charity law and so is free to trade more or less like any commercial company. So long as the trading company donates its profits to the charity under the gift aid scheme (see 12.1), the net result is broadly the same in terms of tax as if the charity had been allowed to carry out the trade tax free itself. In short, no corporation tax will be paid and all the profits can be passed to the charity.

Any profits the trading company retains will (subject to the availability of other set-offs and reliefs) be subject to corporation tax. It may be necessary to take professional advice on this. For example, it may be prudent for the company to build up reserves and capital for expansion, without having to rely on the charity (see below). It may need to repay loans from the charity (or bank) and will only be able to do this out of (usually) taxed profits.

Trading through a separate limited company in this way has the added advantage that it will insulate the charity's funds against the risk of something going wrong with the trade, and the trading company's liability will normally be limited by law to the extent of its own assets. A charity should, however, take care not to put this insulation at risk by indiscriminately allowing the trading company to use its name, logo and style as a come-on, for example, in mail order sales to the public. This could enable creditors to sue the charity for holding itself out as the trader.

Can the charity finance its trading company?

Strictly speaking, the charity can only use its funds to pursue its objects or to invest as its constitution and the law allows (see 8.9). If a charity wants to establish a wholly-owned trading company it should make sure from the outset that its constitution permits such investment.

Similarly, if the trading company is going to need loan facilities, the investment powers of the charity should make it clear that the trustees can make such loans. Such a loan must also be justifiable on normal commercial criteria and trustees cannot blithely assume the trading venture is bound to succeed. Charity Commission guidance requires any such loan to be made at a commercial rate of interest, to be secured on the trading company's assets (though they may not hold much value) and for repayment terms to be clear and complied with.

It is often advisable to get clearance from HMRC where a charity wants to make loans or invest in shares in the subsidiary company, to ensure there is no danger that it will start to lose some of its tax exemptions according to complex tax law tests (on which advice is indispensable if a dispute arises). HMRC needs to be satisfied that the loan or investment in shares is to be made 'for the benefit of the charity and not for the avoidance of tax (whether by the charity or any other person)'. However, loans to and investments in trading companies are generally not considered to be for the avoidance of tax (see 12.2).

As to the prudence of making loans, the need for repayment needs to be considered. It is not within the power of trustees to avoid the embarrassment of their trading company going bust by giving it further loans. However, the terms for loans can be realistic in all the circumstances. That is to say, as long as the package of conditions looks commercially reasonable from the standpoint of a lender and a borrower in such a close relationship (bearing in mind that the trading company will, hopefully, not only repay the loan, but also yield great benefits to the charity in the form of gift aided profits – see 12.1) all should be well.

The charity can also take account of the trading company undertaking expenditures that advance the charity's purposes. But given that repayment of the loan can only come out of the trading company's profits after tax, expert advice should be taken, especially if the loan would represent a significant part of the charity's free assets.

Because of these complications and the overheads and distractions of policing a trading company owned by the charity, it may be best to put what trade the charity can properly undertake itself through the charity.

Separation of the charity and trading company

If a charity sets up a separate trading company on the lines mentioned above, it is vital that the activities of the two are kept separate. What is more, since the charity generally cannot trade as a principal objective, it will be a breach of its constitution for its funds to be used simply to subsidise the trading company. It is also vital to realise that the charity and trading company are not only different legal entities, but are also of a different legal nature and must, therefore, deal with each other at arm's length. For example, a charity should not speculate via its trading company in a way it could not itself speculate, such as by making loans to it to invest in highly speculative money market instruments.

As to administration, insofar as the two organisations share premises, staff and facilities, the expenses, rents and wages involved should be fairly divided so that there is no hidden subsidy of the trading company by the charity.

One safe way of doing this is to keep time records if one of the charity's employees spends normal working hours on trading company business. The rate to be charged should, of course, take account of overheads. Shared premises can be dealt with on a square footage basis, not forgetting, once again, to charge the trading company a fair proportion of the cost of common parts (such as corridors or lifts) and other overheads such as insurance.

Value added tax

A charity's money-earning activities may involve it in making or receiving supplies which give rise to a VAT liability (see 12.2). Broadly, this will be the case where the activity in question involves a supply of goods or services in the UK in the course of a business.

The concept of 'business' is far wider than that of trade (e.g. no profit motive is required). It may include, therefore, the provision of services by a charity to those it seeks to benefit in accordance with its objects (e.g. providing residential care for older and sick people).

In recent years there have been major changes in tax laws vis-à-vis charities. Exemptions are now better than any in the world, except perhaps the USA. Anti-abuse measures are, properly, strict and HMRC VAT inspectors are vigilant.

12 Charities and tax

12.1   Tax efficient giving to charities

Gift aid

Gifts of any amount of cash to charities are eligible for relief under the gift aid scheme, whether made regularly or as a one-off payment.

This enables the charity to recover from HM Revenue and Customs (HMRC) the income tax at the basic rate on the amount of the gift, for which the donor is obliged to account to the HMRC. The effect is to divert the tax from the state to the charity so the donor knows that the true amount of his or her gift includes the basic rate tax, which the charity will recover. In addition, donors who are higher rate tax payers are entitled to relief against the higher rate in respect of gift aided payments.

So, for example, if I intend to pay £100 gross to a charity, I will pay the charity £78 and account to HMRC for basic rate tax of £22, which the charity will recover. If I am a higher rate tax payer (currently payable at 40%) I will not have to pay the extra tax (currently £18). Thus the charity will receive £100 at a real cost to me of £60.

NB: These are current rates, the basic rate of tax will be reduced to 20% from April 2008, though recovery will still be at 22p until 5 April 2011.

Donors must make a gift aid declaration, which is given to the charity so that HMRC is able to audit the relief claimed. Declarations can be made in writing, electronically (over the Internet) or orally. The charity or donor can decide the form of the declaration, provided it includes the following basic information:

- the donor's name and address;
- the charity's name;
- the date and a description of the donation to which the declaration relates;
- a declaration that the donation is to be treated as a gift aid donation;
- a note explaining the requirement that the donor must pay an amount of tax equal to the tax deducted from his or her donation.

Oral declarations are not effective until the charity has sent the donor a written record of the donation that includes a note explaining the donor's entitlement to cancel the declaration retrospectively, or provided the charity keeps an audible and auditable recording of the oral gift aid declaration.

Companies can also claim relief under the gift aid scheme against corporation tax. They are not, however, obliged to account for the tax due to HMRC, nor to make a gift aid declaration in respect of their donations.

The separate tax relief for deeds of covenant was withdrawn with effect from 6 April 2000, but future payments made under existing covenants will still be eligible for relief under the gift aid scheme.

Crucially, a gift is not a gift for tax purposes if the donor receives a significant benefit in return. Where gift aid is concerned, the relevant legislation specifies the maximum benefits that donors (or any person closely connected to them) can receive in return for their donations without loss of gift aid relief.

These rules are important for charities with members who receive benefits as a result of paying their subscriptions.

Providing free or reduced price admission to a charity property is disregarded under these rules if:

- the property's preservation is the charity's sole or main aim; or
- it is to view wildlife whose conservation is the charity's sole or main aim; and
- the same opportunity is available to the public generally in return for a donation;
- the donor either pays at least 10% more than the usual admission price or is allowed annual entry in return for the donation.

Payroll giving

Under the payroll giving scheme employees can authorise their employer to deduct donations to charity from their wages before income tax is deducted under PAYE. This means that income tax relief is given at the top rate at which the employee pays tax.

Any amount can be given under the scheme. The government undertook to pay a 10% supplement on all payroll donations from 5 April 2000 to 6 April 2004.

To help you take advantage of this excellent opportunity, advice on the scheme and the supplement is available from the Charities Aid Foundation's Payroll Services Unit (see appendix 1).

Gifts of shares and securities

Gifts and part gifts (where shares etc. are provided for some payment, but not at market value) of certain shares and securities to charities qualify for complete income tax relief for the donor, equal to market value given away. This is in addition to relief from capital gains tax (explained below). But note, shares and securities in unquoted companies do not qualify.

Gifts of shares and securities to a charity by a company will qualify for full relief from corporation tax.

Other tax free gifts

Certain business payments count as business expenses and are therefore fully deductible in calculating corporation tax. In outline, these are donations for technical education conducted at approved institutes and for approved scientific research, and smallish gifts to local charities under the HMRC extra statutory concession B7. In each case, the education, research or charity project must be related to the trade of the business.

Certain gifts to schools and universities of trading stock and other articles and plant used in the course of carrying out a trade by a business are tax deductible. So are gifts in kind of articles manufactured or sold by the donor.

Traders may donate other goods and services to charities on a tax deductible basis, although there is a specific relieving provision for the costs involved in seconding an employee to a charity on a temporary basis. This can, however, have VAT consequences. Take advice.

Also note that gifts or part gifts which can be justified as, for example, public relations expenditure, are tax deductible.

Capital gains tax

Gifts to charities of assets that are 'pregnant' with capital gains (i.e. have a base value increased by capital gains) are entirely free of tax in spite of the fact that the disposal would otherwise be a disposal for tax purposes by the donor. There is no limit to this exemption, which is a valuable one.

Inheritance tax

Inheritance tax is chargeable on lifetime gifts (at 20%) and on the value of a person's estate when they die (at 40%), although there is a sizeable tax free band of £300,000, rising to £325,000 from April 2009.

Gifts to charity of any amount, whether made in life or on death, are completely exempt from inheritance tax. That is to say, the assets given away are taken completely out of the donor's estate for inheritance tax purposes and of course the charity pays nothing.

If, however, the gift is complicated by having conditions attached to it – it is postponed in effect, is for a limited period, entitles the donor to some benefit out of the gift, or is paid out of a trust – then some inheritance tax may be payable. Seek advice from a solicitor or accountant.

Non-resident donors

A donor who is not resident in the UK for tax purposes and who wants to make tax efficient gifts to a UK charity can do so under the gift aid scheme, provided he or she has income or capital gains which are chargeable to UK tax. The tax deducted from the gift and reclaimed by the charity cannot exceed the tax otherwise payable by the donor.

Alternatively, a non-UK resident donor may be able to make the gift to a cooperative intermediate charity in his or her country of residence to obtain whatever tax concessions are available there for charitable donations. In this, as in so many other matters concerning tax, professional guidance is likely to be essential.

12.2   Charities and tax relief

Income and corporation tax

There is no single exemption from income and corporation tax for charities. There is, instead, a wide range of exemptions in respect of most (but not all) of the different types of income charities may receive, such as dividends, bank interest and rent.

These exemptions are detailed in section 505 of the Income and Corporation Taxes Act 1988 and will only be granted insofar as the income in question is applied solely for the charity's objects (see chapter 11). 'Applied' does not mean that the charity must use or spend the income in the same year as it is received. It can intentionally be accumulated.

Loss of tax exemptions

HMRC is highly concerned about the tiny minority of people who abuse these generous charity tax exemptions, for example avoiding corporation tax by covenanting profits to a 'captive' charity which misuses the funds, or trustees allowing non-charitable expenditure.

Anti-abuse regulations are far reaching and if a charity falls foul of them it will lose its tax exemptions.

The following categories of charity will have nothing to worry about.

* Charities whose relevant income and gains (RIGs) for the year concerned are less than £10,000. RIGs include covenanted income, dividends, interest, capital gains, rents, one-off gifts by companies, gift aid donations, gifts from other charities and profits of any trade carried on by the charity.

- Charities that:
  - make no non-qualifying investments or loans (mainly those to private companies for which approval has not been obtained from HMRC);
  - do not incur any non-qualifying expenditure (i.e. do not misapply their funds, for example by making non-charitable payments or donations).
- Surprisingly, even charities which cannot bring themselves within the above conditions (because, for example, they have misspent funds) will nonetheless keep their tax exemptions if their proper (that is to say qualifying) charitable expenditure (on grants, expenses incurred in running the charity and finance charges) exceed their RIGs for the year.

So, only those charities not able to bring themselves within one of these categories in any year will be in danger of losing tax relief. They will almost certainly need professional advice.

It is important to note the following.

- Where charities lose their tax exemptions the trustees or directors may be personally liable if improper expenditures are the cause.
- The HMRC guide on the tax advantages of being a charity is very helpful (see appendix 2).
- Special clearance is needed for overseas grants as well as certain loans and investments.
- Qualifying expenditure includes commitments of a non-contractual, as well as a contractual, nature (even where there may not have been an actual payment in the period of account).

Capital gains tax

Charities pay no capital gains tax on the receipt of gifts or on the sale of their assets (subject to the anti-abuse measures, which need not concern the innocent).

It is often sensible, therefore, for a person who wishes to make a gift (which would otherwise give rise to a significant capital gain) to transfer the asset itself to the charity. That will be tax free (see above) and if and when the charity sells the asset, the proceeds will be free of tax.

Stamp duty

Charities are exempt from stamp duty land tax (SDLT) on all acquisitions of interest in land, whether by gift or purchase. SDLT was introduced on 1

December 2003. It makes stamp duty on land transactions more like mainstream tax and requires a tax return to be completed within 30 days. The charities exemption has to be claimed in the return, and the relief is subject to two conditions:

(a) the charity must intend to hold the property for qualifying charitable purposes;

(b) the transaction must not have been entered into to avoid SDLT.

The relief may be withdrawn within three years if the charity ceases to be established for charitable purposes or the property ceases to be used for charitable purposes. The extent of the withdrawal and consequential obligation to pay SDLT will depend on the circumstances.

Outright gifts of shares to a charity will not generate a stamp duty charge.

Value added tax

As indicated earlier (see chapter 11) there is no general exemption from VAT for charities. They can, however, benefit from a patchwork of exemptions and zero rated supplies.

Generally, charities with taxable supplies (i.e. goods and services supplied by them for which they charge) of more than £67,000 a year (2008/09 figure) (towards which zero rated, but not exempt, supplies count – see below) must register for VAT with HMRC within 30 days of the end of the month when the limit was reached. If your taxable supplies are under £67,000 you neither have to register, nor charge VAT on them.

Exempt supplies

These include:

* the provision of education or research by educational establishments and professional training by charities;
* providing care, treatment or instruction to promote the welfare of older, ill, distressed or disabled people;
* goods and services closely linked to the protection of children and young people;
* goods and services provided by a charity in connection with small-scale fundraising events (the rules are identical to those which offer exemption from tax – see 11.3).

Zero rated supplies

These include:

- sales of talking books for blind and disabled people and wireless sets for blind people;
- sales of equipment for the relief of chronically sick and disabled people;
- the sale of donated goods in charity shops;
- the export of goods by a charity.

Generally, none of these exempt or zero rated supplies must be supplied other than by or for charities or public bodies.

This is a complex, technical subject. Further information is available from the Revenue and Customs Call Centre (see appendix 1), NCVO's excellent, detailed guide, the *VAT Guide for Charities*, and the Charities Tax Reform Group (see appendices 1 and 2).

Beware! Where members of a charity pay subscriptions and receive benefits in return there is both a tax danger (see 12.1) and a VAT danger. Take advice.

Irrecoverable VAT

It is often wrongly assumed that charities, like most businesses, can recover VAT on their costs by completing a VAT return for HMRC. However, where their sales are exempt from VAT, EU law prohibits them from recovering VAT on their costs. VAT is therefore an additional cost for the majority of charities.

Rates (non-domestic property)

Non-domestic property is subject to the rating system introduced by the Local Government Finance Act 1988. This introduced three categories of rate relief.

- Where the property is used for religious worship (a certificate is needed except in respect of the Church of England or the Church of Wales) or for disabled people (training or welfare or other facilities) there is complete exemption from rates.
- Where the property is 'wholly or mainly used for charitable purposes' (which includes premises so used by a charity – not its trading company – for the sale of donated goods) mandatory 80% relief is

available. The local council also has discretion to relieve the remaining 20%.

- Where the property is wholly or mainly used by a not-for-profit recreational organisation or occupied by a not-for-profit philanthropic, social welfare, educational, religious, scientific, literary or fine arts organisation, the council has complete discretion to relieve the organisation from rates.

Council tax (domestic property)

Council tax replaced the short-lived and notorious poll tax. It is property based, and will apply to charitable and voluntary domestic property if it can be defined as a 'dwelling'.

The council tax has two elements – a property part and a personal part. It is complicated, with 23 categories of property (mostly unoccupied ones) entitled to exemption and nine groups of people who can be 'disregarded' in assessing liability (the assumption being that each household will comprise an average of two adults, with a 25% discount allowable where there is only one and 50% if there are none). Exempt dwellings include, for example, university halls of residence. Disregarded groups include, for example, severely learning disabled people, long-stay hospital patients, students, patients in nursing and residential care homes and care workers. Further, a property owned or leased by a registered charity will qualify for an exemption of up to six months whilst it is unoccupied. Charities should seek specific advice on liability. Start with the local authority or a relevant advice-giving body.

12.3   'Personal' charities

Individuals or companies can often be encouraged to give more to charity if they set up their own 'personal' charity. One of the most pleasurable secondary motives for many individuals and companies in giving to charity is the thought that tax on hard-earned income and gains can in effect be diverted from HMRC to a charity on the coat-tails of the gift!

The constitution of the personal charity can be relatively simple and provide maximum scope for the trustees as regards objects, investments and decision making. One can only make tax exempt gift aid payments to an established charity. The charity itself, however, can give for charitable purposes. This would allow it, for example, to make a grant to a non-charity or an individual so long as it was clearly earmarked, accepted and spent by that non-charity or individual for a charitable project or purpose.

This can be simply arranged in advance with the donor. It could, for example, cover books or equipment for a needy individual, or money or a holiday.

Another advantage of the personal charity is that the person setting it up can be a trustee with his or her nearest and dearest, although the Charity Commission prefers at least one trustee from outside the founder's immediate family. Where a company sets up a charity, however, it is usually perfectly satisfactory to confine trustees to directors and/or shareholders and/or employees.

Having established a personal charity, the founder, whether company or individual, makes gift aid gifts to it. Each year the charity's trustees recover the tax and decide, with full flexibility, how to dispense this charitable money.

13 Politics and campaigning

13.1 Introduction

Charities are not permitted to have directly political objects and there is nothing in the Charities Act 2006 that changes this. Charities are therefore restricted in the nature and extent of their campaigning work. In March 2008, the Commission published a revised version of its guidance *Campaigning and Political Activities by Charities* (CC9). The reason for the revision was to address confusion that previous guidance appeared to be causing to some charities, leading some to be unnecessarily cautious, rather than any change to the underlying legal principles.

What remains clear is that a body that has objects expressly to change the law in some way cannot be registered as a charity. Further, regardless of its objects, if the main weight of a charity's activity is directed towards changing the law it will probably be acting outside charitable limits. But that still leaves ample scope.

13.2 Permissible political activity

Campaigning activities which can further charitable purposes are allowed; these include campaigning activity that aims to ensure existing laws are observed. Also allowed are political activities undertaken only in the context of supporting charitable purposes. Examples of the type of political activity a charity is allowed to carry out are:

- providing information, advice and reasoned comment when this is requested by MPs, ministers or government officials;
- making balanced, rational comment on green or white papers;
- providing members of either House of Parliament with non-partisan information, advice and reasoned argument, especially from the charity's on-ground experience, for or against a published bill and any amendments. It may even draft amendments relevant to its objects and in relation to current political concerns or debate;

- lobbying members to support its cause in Parliament, for instance, where the question arises whether a government grant is to be made or continued to a particular charity or country whose poor it seeks to help;
- carrying on some non party-political parliamentary activity, for example supporting enabling legislation that will grant a charity wider scope to carry out its purposes;
- educating the public in a rational way concerning the needs it meets and ways of ameliorating them, particularly where this derives from the direct experiences of its beneficiaries.

If the political activities you envisage fall outside these categories, they may still be permissible if it is a situation where carrying out political activity is the best way for trustees to support the charity's purposes. A charity may choose to focus most or all of its resources on political activity for a period but these cannot be the only activities it carries out. For example, it may well be lawful for a disaster relief charity to organise a sustained information campaign to persuade the government to intervene with taxpayers' money in some potential or actual overseas tragedy. Similarly, it would be acceptable for a housing charity to canvas for greater allocation of national resources for homeless people.

It is fair to point out, though, that this is sensitive territory for the Charity Commission. Above all, in any political activity a charity should be non-partisan, objective, balanced and fact-based, and strike an appropriate tone.

13.3   Sanctions for excess

If, for example, a charity is found to have engaged in impermissible political activities, the trustees may, in the worst case, be asked to pay to the charity the funds which have been misapplied. The charity may also have to forfeit to HM Revenue and Customs the tax relief on the misapplied funds, but it would not lose its charitable status. That would be to punish the public (for a charity is a public benefit organisation) for the trustees' failings.

13.4   Parallel political organisations

Several charities, realising that some of their proposed activities would fall the wrong side of the shadowy dividing line between what is and what is not permitted by way of political activity, have established separate non-charitable organisations to carry on those functions. On other occasions a non-charitable organisation has hived off its charitable activities. Examples include Liberty and Friends of the Earth. In such cases it is up to the charity to avoid confusion between the two bodies.

The Charity Commission is sometimes uneasy that this separation of the two parallel organisations may in practice degenerate into a single muddle. It is essential to prepare the ground thoroughly so that the mechanics of cost apportionment and cross-accounting between the two bodies have been properly resolved and are duly implemented.

13.5 Education and propaganda

The distinction between public education, which is permitted to charities, and propaganda, which isn't, is sometimes a fine one. A vigorous campaign run by a charity to inform the public of its beneficiaries' needs should be acceptable so long as people are objectively informed, unless the charity is merely advancing an ideological solution to a problem. This then strays into propaganda, lacking the necessary rationality and balance.

13.6 Think tanks

In recent years a number of charitable research organisations have been very active, such as the (rightish) Adam Smith Institute and Institute of Economic Affairs and the (leftish) Institute for Public Policy Research. In the light of the sensitivity occasionally manifested on Parliament's back benches against 'politicking' by charities, it is perhaps not surprising that the Charity Commission has been asked to look at the status of think tanks. They manage to stay inside the ropes by having diverse great and good on their committees and maintaining some semblance of political balance in their programmes of work.

13.7 General conclusions

Charities that find themselves butting against these hazy frontiers when trying to do the best by their charitable purposes are highly advised to develop a protocol of 'dos and don'ts' for their staff and supporters. This can prevent misunderstanding, or worse.

In practice the Charity Commission is patient with established charities over any quasi-political activities they undertake. This sensitive area of charity practice is one in which a good deal of tact and restraint has thus far avoided too many collisions.

Appendix 1

USEFUL CONTACTS

acevo (The Association of Chief Executive Officers of Voluntary Organisations)

1 New Oxford Street, London WC1A 1NU

Tel: 0845 345 8481; fax: 0845 345 8482; email: info@acevo.org.uk; website: www.acevo.org.uk

Runs training and induction programmes and coordinates a network for members to share expertise.

Architectural Heritage Fund

Alhambra House, 27–31 Charing Cross Road, London WC2H 0AU

Tel: 020 7925 0199; fax: 020 7930 0295; email: ahf@ahfund.org.uk; website: www.ahfund.org.uk

Provides advice and funding in relation to architectural heritage projects. Can provide a model constitution for architectural heritage trusts.

Action with Communities in Rural England (ACRE)

Somerford Court, Somerford Road, Cirencester, Gloucestershire GL7 1TW

Tel: 01285 653477; fax: 01285 654537; email: acre@acre.org.uk; website: www.acre.org.uk

Provides information and advice on rural community development and setting up projects to support local action.

Arts Council England

14 Great Peter Street, London SW1P 3NQ

Tel: 0845 300 6200; textphone: 020 7973 6564; fax: 020 7973 6590; email: enquiries@artscouncil.org.uk; website: www.artscouncil.org.uk

The main channel for distribution of government money for the arts. Its information unit can provide model constitutions for arts groups.

Arts & Business

Nutmeg House, 60 Gainsford Street, Butler's Wharf, London SE1 2NY
Tel: 020 7378 8143; fax: 020 7407 7527; email: head.office@AandB.org.uk;
website: www.aandb.org.uk

Promotes, and provides advice in relation to, business sponsorship of the
arts.

Association of Charitable Foundations

Central House, 14 Upper Woburn Place, London WC1H 0AE
Tel: 020 7255 4499; fax: 020 7255 4496; email: acf@acf.org.uk; website:
www.acf.org.uk

Membership body for grant-making trusts and foundations dedicated to the
promotion of good practice and the encouragement of philanthropic giving.

Association of Charity Officers

Five Ways, 57/59 Halfield Road, Potters Bar, Hertfordshire EN6 1HS
Tel: 01707 651777; fax 01707 660477; email: info@aco.uk.net; website:
www.aco.uk.net

Liaises between, and represents, charities in the welfare and social services
field.

bassac

33 Corsham Street, London N1 6DR
Tel: 0845 241 0375; fax: 0845 241 0376; email: info@bassac.org.uk; website:
www.bassac.org.uk

The national network of multi-purpose organisations that provide services
and community development support and host smaller community
initiatives. Represents them at a national level and provides strategic
support.

Bates Wells & Braithwaite

2–6 Cannon Street, London EC4M 6YH
Tel: 020 7551 7777; fax: 020 7551 7800; email: mail@bwbllp.com; website:
www.bateswells.co.uk

Leading charity law solicitors. The author of this handbook, Julian Blake is a partner at BWB and is particularly involved with the application of corporate/commercial law to charities and social enterprises and the engagement between these organisations and the public sector. This edition follows five previous editions written by Andrew Phillips (Lord Phillips of Sudbury OBE), founder partner of BWB.

Big Lottery Fund

1 Plough Place, London EC4A 1DE
Tel: 020 7211 1800 (general); 0845 410 2030 (advice line); textphone: 0845 039 0204; email: general.enquiries@biglotteryfund.org.uk; website: www.biglotteryfund.org.uk

The largest distributor of Lottery money; created from a merger of the Community Fund and the New Opportunities Fund.

Business in the Community

137 Shepherdess Walk, London N1 7RQ
Tel: 0870 600 2482; fax: 020 7253 1877; email: information@bitc.org.uk; website: www.bitc.org.uk

A national partnership of companies, central and local government, the voluntary sector and trades unions. Promotes corporate responsibility and greater involvement in the community by developing and publicising schemes aimed at job creation.

Central Council for Physical Recreation (CCPR)

Burwood House, 14–16 Caxton Street, London SW1H 0QT
Tel: 020 7976 3900; fax: 020 7976 3901; email: info@ccpr.org.uk; website: www.ccpr.org.uk

The umbrella body for national governing and representative bodies of sports and recreation in the UK.

CaSE Insurance for Charities

aQmen Ltd, James House, Emlyn Lane, Leatherhead, Surrey KT22 7EP
Tel: 0845 225 2288; fax: 0845 225 2295; email: enquiries@aQmen.ltd.uk; website: www.caseinsurance.co.uk

Charities Advisory Trust (CAT)

Radius Works, Back Lane, London NW3 IHL
Tel: 020 7794 9835; fax: 020 7431 3739; email:
people@charitiesadvisorytrust.org.uk; website:
www.charitiesadvisorytrust.co.uk

Provides advice and training on all aspects of charity trading and shops,
including in relation to establishing trading subsidiaries.

Charities Aid Foundation (CAF)

25 Kings Hill Avenue, Kings Hill, West Malling, Kent ME19 4TA
Tel: 01732 520000; fax: 01732 520001; email: enquiries@cafonline.org;
website: www.cafonline.org.uk

Promotes the flow of funds to charities, advises on many aspects of
charitable giving and fundraising, gives information on grant-making trusts
and provides financial services to charities and charity supporters.

Charities Tax Reform Group

Church House, Great Smith Street, London SWIP 3AZ
Tel: 020 7222 1265; fax: 020 7222 1250; email: info@ctrg.org.uk; website:
www.ctrg.org.uk

A campaigning organisation dedicated to seeking tax and VAT reforms for
charities and concerned with charity law reform in these areas.

Charity Bank

PO Box 398, 194 High Street, Tonbridge, Kent TN9 9BD
Tel: 01732 774040; fax: 01732 774069; email: enquiries@charitybank.org;
website: www.charitybank.org

A charitable bank established by CAF (see above). Supports charities by
providing loans on beneficial terms, particularly to organisations in
disadvantaged communities.

Charity Commission for England and Wales

Charity Commission Direct, PO Box 1227, Liverpool L69 3UG
Tel: 0845 3000 218; textphone 0845 3000 219; fax: 0151 703 1555;
website: www.charity-commission.gov.uk

Regulates charities in England and Wales; maintains a searchable register of registered charities; provides advice, information and publications on many charity law issues.

Charity Finance Directors Group

3rd Floor, Downstream Building, 1 London Bridge, London SE1 9BG
Tel: 0845 345 3192; fax: 0845 345 3193; email: info@cfdg.org.uk; website: www.cfdg.org.uk

A membership organisation for charity finance directors. Organises seminars on financial and accounting matters.

Charity Law Association

c/o Catherine Rustomji, Honorary Secretary, Dickinson Dees LLP, Camden House, Princes Wharf, Teesdale, Stockon-on-Tees TS17 6QY
Tel: 01642 631261; email catherine.rustomji@dickinson-dees.com; website: www.charitylawassociation.org.uk

An association of lawyers and others interested in charity law issues.

Charity Trustee Network

3–4 Frensham Suite, Friary Court, 13–21 High Street, Guildford GU1 3DG
Tel: 01483 230280; fax: 01483 303932; email: info@trusteenet.org.uk; website: www.trusteenet.org.uk

Promotes mutual support among, and provides information to, charity trustees.

Charter Mark Team

Government Communications, Policy Projects Team, 22/26 Whitehall, London SW1A 2WH
Tel: 020 7276 1720; email: chartermark@cabinet-office.x.gsi.gov.uk; website: www.cabinetoffice.gov.uk/chartermark

Implements the Charter Mark scheme, which recognises high standards for organisations (including voluntary) that provide direct services to the public.

Citizens Advice

Myddleton House, 115–123 Pentonville Road, London N1 9LZ
Tel: 020 7833 2181 (admin only); fax 020 7833 4371; website:
www.citizensadvice.org.uk

The national body for citizens advice bureaux (CABx), responsible for CAB
policy and the nationwide provision of a free independent service for the
public.

Civic Trust

Essex Hall, 1–6 Essex Street, London WC2R 3HU
Tel: 020 7539 7900; fax: 020 7539 7901; email: info@civictrust.org.uk;
website: www.civictrust.org.uk

Dedicated to improving and regenerating the urban environment. Local
environment groups may register. Also provides model constitutions and
guidance for groups such as local historical associations and conservation
societies.

Commission for the Compact

77 Paradise Circus, Queensway, Birmingham B1 2DT
Tel: 0121 237 5900; fax: 0121 233 2120; email info@thecompact.org.uk;
website: www.thecompact.org.uk

Work includes developing an evidence base on the Compact's progress,
sharing good practice and looking thematically at key themes that affect the
relationship between statutory and voluntary sectors. Also promotes and
reviews the policy and operation of the Compact and its codes, nationally
and locally.

Companies House

Crown Way, Maindy, Cardiff CF14 3UZ
Tel: 0870 33 33 636; minicom: 02920 381245; email: enquiries@companies-
house.gov.uk; website: www.companieshouse.gov.uk

Regulates companies. Maintains a searchable register of companies and
provides information and advice.

Community Matters

12–20 Baron Street, London N1 9LL
Tel: 020 7837 7887; fax: 020 7278 9253; email:
communitymatters@communitymatters.org.uk; website:
www.communitymatters.org.uk

Represents the interests of local community organisations and offers
information, advice and practical help to local community groups. Provides a
model constitution suitable for use by such groups.

Criminal Records Bureau (CRB)

CRB Customer Services, PO Box 110, Liverpool, L69 3EF
Tel: 0870 90 90 811; minicom: 0870 90 90 344; website: www.crb.gov.uk

Helps organisations in the public, private and voluntary sectors by identifying
candidates who may be unsuitable to work with children or other
vulnerable members of society, checking police records and, in relevant
cases, information held by the Department of Health and the Department
for Children, Schools and Families.

Development Trusts Association

33 Corsham Street, London N1 6DR
Tel: 0845 158 8336; fax: 0845 458 8337; email: info@dta.org.uk; website:
www.dta.org.uk

A community-based regeneration network for information sharing and
network building between development trusts in different communities.

Directory of Social Change

24 Stephenson Way, London NW1 2DP
website: www.dsc.org.uk

Publications: tel: 08450 77 77 07; fax: 020 7391 4804; email:
books@dsc.org.uk

Courses and conferences: tel: 08450 77 77 07; fax 020 7391 4808; email:
training@dsc.org.uk

Northern office: Federation House, Hope Street, Liverpool L1 9BW
Tel: 0151 708 0117 fax: 0151 708 0136; email: north@dsc.org.uk

The Directory of Social Change is an independent voice for positive social change, set up in 1975 to help voluntary organisations become more effective. We do this by providing practical, challenging and affordable information and training to meet the current, emerging and future needs of the sector. Our main activities include researching and publishing reference guides and handbooks, providing practical training courses, and running conferences and briefing sessions.

Equality and Human Rights Commission

3 More London, Riverside, Tooley Street, London SE1 3RG
Tel: 020 5117 0235; fax: 01925 884 275; email:
info@equalityhumanrights.com; www.equalityhumanrights.com

Works to eliminate discrimination, reduce inequality, protect human rights and build good relations, ensuring that everyone has a fair chance in society. Incorporates the Equal Opportunities Commission, the Commission for Racial Equality and the Disability Rights Commission. Has a directorate of specialist equality law lawyers.

Ethical Investment Research Services (EIRIS)

80–84 Bondway, London SW8 1SF
Tel: 020 7840 5700; fax 020 7735 5323; email: ethics@eiris.org; website:
www.eiris.org

A charity dedicated to providing information to assist investors invest in accordance with their principles. Measures UK and international companies against a range of ethical criteria.

Financial Services Authority

Mutual Societies Registration Unit, Authorisation Division, 8th Floor, The North Colonnade, Canary Wharf, London E14 5HS
Tel: 020 7066 1000; email: mutual.societies@fsa.gov.uk; website:
www.fsa.gov.uk/Pages/Doing/Small_firms/MSR/index.shtml

Responsible for the registration and regulation of friendly societies and industrial and provident societies.

Fundraising Standards Board

Hampton House, Albert Embankment, London SE1 7TJ
Tel: 0845 402 5442; fax: 0845 402 5443; email: info@frsb.org.uk; website:
www.frsb.org.uk

Implements and oversees a transparent self-regulatory scheme for
fundraising in the UK. Encourages high standards in fundraising and works to
increase public confidence in charitable giving. Charities that join the
scheme will use the scheme logo to demonstrate their commitment, which
is underpinned by a robust and accessible complaints procedure for
members of the public should they have a problem.

Gambling Commission

Victoria Square House, Victoria Square, Birmingham B2 4BP
Tel: 0121 230 6500; fax: 0121 237 6720; email:
info@gamblingcommission.gov.uk; website: www.gamblingcommission.gov.uk

Regulatory body providing licences, certificates of consent and registrations
for gaming and lotteries. Also provides information and advice.

Health and Safety Commission and Executive

Rose Court, 2 Southwark Bridge, London SE1 9HS

HSE Infoline, Caerphilly Business Park, Caerphilly CF83 3GG
Tel: HSE Infoline: 0845 345 0055; fax: 0845 408 9566; email:
hse.infoline@natbrit.com; website: www.hse.gov.uk

Enforces health and safety standards and provides guidance, advice, research
and an information service.

HM Revenue and Customs Contact Centre

National Advice Service, Written Enquiries Section, Alexander House,
Victoria Avenue, Southend on Sea, Essex SS99 1BD
Tel: 0845 010 9000; textphone: 0845 000 0200; email:
enquiries.estn@hmrc.gsi.gov.uk; website: www.hmrc.gov.uk

Provides advice, forms, notices and publications re former Customs and
Excise taxes and duties (including VAT).

HM Revenue and Customs Charities

St John's House, Merton Road, Bootle, Merseyside L69 9BB
Tel: 08453 02 02 03; website: www.hmrc.gov.uk/charities

Responsible for all matters relating to the taxation of charities, including
VAT and VAT reliefs. Also covers community amateur sports clubs.

Housing Corporation

Maple House, 149 Tottenham Court Road, London WIT 7BN
Tel: 0845 230 7000; fax: 020 7393 2111; website: www.housingcorp.gov.uk

Has responsibility for investing public money in housing associations and
regulating the housing association sector in the interests of residents.

HSE Books

PO Box 1999, Sudbury, Suffolk CO10 2WA
Tel: 01787 881 165; fax: 01787 313995; email: hsebooks@prolog.uk.com;
website: www.hsebooks.co.uk

Provides direct order service for Health and Safety Executive publications,
leaflets and books (some of which are free of charge).

Information Commission

Wycliffe House, Water Lane, Wilmslow, Cheshire SK9 5AF
Tel: 01625 54 57 45 or 08456 30 60 60; fax: 01625 525 510; email:
notification@ico.gsi.gov.uk (for enquiries about notification); website:
www.ico.gov.uk

Supervisory authority in relation to data protection. Duties include the
promotion of good information handling and providing codes of practice for
data controllers.

Institute of Fundraising

Park Place, 12 Lawn Lane, London SW8 1UD
Tel: 020 7840 1000; fax: 020 7840 1001; email: enquiries@institute-of-
fundraising.org.uk website: www.institute-of-fundraising.org.uk

The professional body representing and supporting fundraisers. Promotes
standards of fundraising practice.

Interchange Studios

Hampstead Town Hall Centre, 213 Haverstock Hill, London NW3 4QP
Tel: 020 7692 5800; fax: 020 7692 5801; email:
bookings@interchange.org.uk; website: www.interchange.org.uk

Services include education for disadvantaged young people (through the
performing arts), facilities for disabled children and young people, legal
advice and training to charities and facilities for community groups.

Investors in People

7–10 Chandos Street, London W1G 9DQ
Tel: 020 7467 1900; fax: 020 7636 2386; email: information@iipuk.co.uk;
website: www.investorsinpeople.co.uk

Awards the national quality standard for improving an organisation's
performance through its people. Provides advice, assessment services and
information on best practice

The Legislation Monitoring Service for Charities

Church House, Great Smith Street, London SW1P 3AZ
Tel: 020 7222 1265; fax: 020 7222 1250; email: info@lmsconline.org;
website: www.lmsconline.org

Provides a regular bulletin (ten/year) giving information on current and
proposed legislation and policy developments in the UK and Europe that
may affect charities.

National Association for Voluntary and Community Action (NAVCA)

The Tower, 2 Furnival Square, Sheffield S1 4QL
Tel: 0114 278 6636; textphone: 0114 278 7025; fax: 0114 278 7004; email:
navca@navca.org.uk; website: www.navca.org.uk

A membership organisation that helps promote voluntary and community
action by supporting member councils for voluntary service and acting as a
national voice for the local voluntary and community sector.

National Council for Voluntary Organisations (NCVO)

Regent's Wharf, 8 All Saints Street, London N1 9RL
Tel: 020 7713 6161; textphone: 0800 01 88 111; fax 020 7713 6300;

helpdesk 0800 2 798 798; email: ncvo@ncvo-vol.org.uk; website: www.ncvo-vol.org.uk

Lobbies, represents collective views of members, provides information and advice and produces publications on issues affecting the voluntary sector.

National Housing Federation

Lion Court, 25 Procter Street, London WC1V 6NY
Tel: 020 7067 1010; fax: 020 7067 1011; email: london@housing.org.uk; website: www.housing.org.uk

Advises, and makes representations on behalf of, housing associations. Will help housing associations that use its model rules register as industrial and provident societies.

Northern Ireland Council of Voluntary Action

61 Duncairn Gardens, Belfast BT15 2GB
Tel: 028 9087 7777; minicom: 028 9087 7776; fax: 028 9087 7799; email: nicva@nicva.org; website: www.nicva.org

The umbrella body for voluntary organisations in Northern Ireland, where it has a similar role to NCVO.

Office of the Third Sector

35 Great Smith Street, London SW1P 3BQ
Tel: 020 7276 6400; website: www.cabinetoffice.gov.uk/third_sector

Government department, based within the Cabinet Office, which works with the voluntary sector. Deals with charity law and regulation affecting charities in England and Wales. Responsible for the reform of charity law, monitoring new legislation and changes to existing legislation and laws governing public charitable collections.

Scottish Council for Voluntary Organisations (SCVO)

The Mansfield Traquair Centre, 15 Mansfield Place, Edinburgh EH3 6BB
Tel: 0131 556 3882; fax: 0131 556 0279; email: enquiries@scvo.org.uk; website: www.scvo.org.uk

The umbrella body for voluntary organisations in Scotland, where it has a similar role to NCVO.

Volunteering England

Regent's Wharf, 8 All Saints Street, London N1 9RL
Tel: 0845 305 6979; fax: 020 7520 8910; email:
volunteering@volunteering.org.uk; website: www.volunteering.org.uk

Promotes volunteering with the aim of increasing its quality, quantity, contribution and accessibility.

Wales Council for Voluntary Action

Baltic House, Mount Stuart Square, Cardiff Bay, Cardiff CF10 5FH
Tel: 029 20431700; minicom: 029 20431702; fax: 029 20431701; email:
enquiries@wcva.org.uk; website: www.wcva.org.uk

The umbrella body for voluntary organisations in Wales, where it has a similar role to NCVO.

UK Social Investment Forum

Holywell Centre, 1 Phipp Street, London EC2A 4PS
Tel: 020 7749 9950; email: info@uksif.org; website: www.uksif.org

Promotes and encourages socially responsible investment in the UK.

Appendix 2

USEFUL PUBLICATIONS

Bates Wells & Braithwaite

Jordans Charities Administration Service (loose-leaf), contributors include Stephen Lloyd, Julian Blake, Rosamund Smith and Philip Kirkpatrick, published by Jordans, 1999, £165, ISBN 0 85308 327 4 (available from www.jordanpublishing.co.uk)

Charities – The New Law 2006: A Practical Guide to the Charities Acts, Stephen Lloyd (and others), published by Jordans, 2007, £39, ISBN 978 0 85308 971 1 (available from www.jordanpublishing.co.uk)

Duties of Charity Trustees, 2006, (downloadable at www.bwbllp.com or available direct from Bates Wells and Braithwaite)

The Fundraiser's Guide to the Law, contributors include Stephen Lloyd, Christine Rigby, Philip Kirkpatrick & Rosamund Smith, published by the Directory of Social Change, 2000, £19.95, ISBN 1 900360 78 0

Guidelines for Governance: Information Manual, £25.00 (available direct from Bates, Wells & Braithwaite)

Directory of Social Change

DSC also publishes a number of other books, on fundraising (including regional funding guides), management, finance and the law. All prices were correct at the time of going to press. Publications can be ordered from DSC's website: www.dsc.org.uk or call 08450 77 77 07 for a free catalogue (or download one from the website).

Boards that Work: A Guide for Charity Trustees, David Fishel, 2003, £19.95, ISBN 1 903991 16 1

Budget Yourselves, free budgeting software on the FunderFinder website: www.funderfinder.org.uk and click on 'our software'

The Charity Treasurer's Handbook (2nd edn), Gareth G Morgan, 2008, £12.95, ISBN 1 900360 89 6

The Charity Trustee's Handbook, Mike Eastwood, 2001, £12.95,
ISBN 1 900360 88 8

The Complete Fundraising Handbook (5th edn), Nina Botting Herbst &
Michael Norton, published in association with IOF, 2007, £22.95,
ISBN 1 900360 84 8

Data Protection for Voluntary Organisations (3rd edn), Paul Ticher, published
in association with Bates, Wells & Braithwaite, 2002, £18.95,
ISBN 1 903991 19 6

The Directory of Grant Making Trusts 2007/08 (20th edn), Alan French et al,
published in association with Charities Aid Foundation, 2007, £99.00,
ISBN 1 903991 79 4

The Grant-making Trusts CD-ROM, 2007, published in association with
Charities Aid Foundation, £175 + VAT, ISBN 978 1 903991 83 1

A Guide to the Major Trusts 2007/08 Volume 1 (11th edn), Tom Traynor &
Denise Lillya 2007, £39.95, ISBN 1 903991 77 0

A Guide to the Major Trusts 2007/08 Volume 2 (8th edn), Alan French, Sarah
Johnston & John Smyth, 2007, £39.95, ISBN 1 903991 78 7

The Guide to UK Company Giving 2007/08 (6th edn), John Smyth & Denise
Lillya, 2007, £39.95, ISBN 1 903991 76 3

The Health & Safety Handbook (2nd edn), Al Hinde & Charlie Kavanagh,
edited by Jill Barlow, Published in association with Health @ Work, 2001,
£16.95, ISBN 1 903991 01 3

The Minute Taker's Handbook, Lee Comer & Paul Ticher, 2002, £12.95,
ISBN 1 900360 99 3

A Practical Guide to Charity Accounting: Preparing Charity SORP Accounts, Kate
Sayer (editor), published in association with Sayer Vincent, 2003, £18.95,
ISBN 1 900360 21 8

*A Practical Guide to Financial Management for Charities and Voluntary
Organisations* (3rd edn), Kate Sayer, published in association with Sayer
Vincent, 2007, £18.95, ISBN 1 903991 72 2

A Practical Guide to VAT 2008 for Charities and Voluntary Organisations (3rd
edn), Kate Sayer, published in association with Sayer Vincent, 2008, £18.95,
ISBN 1 900360 91 6

Recruiting Volunteers, Fraser Dyer & Ursula Jost, 2002, £14.95, ISBN 1 903991 20 X

The Russell-Cooke Voluntary Sector Legal Handbook (3rd edn), Sandy Adirondack & James Sinclair Taylor, 2008, £60 (voluntary organisations); £90 (others), ISBN 1 900360 7 21

Voluntary but not Amateur (8th edn), Jacki Reason and Ruth Hayes, 2009

Writing Better Fundraising Applications, (3rd edn) Michael Norton & Mike Eastwood, published in association with the Institute of Fundraising, 2002, £18.95, ISBN 1 903991 09 9

www.trustfunding.org.uk, annual subscription £160 + VAT (Charities and voluntary organisations) £205 + VAT (Statutory and commercial)

Cabinet Office

Private Action, Public Benefit: A Review of Charities and the Wider Not-for-Profit Sector, 2002 (available from the Prime Minister's Strategy Unit – www.cabinetoffice.gov.uk/strategy/publications.aspx)

Public Appointments Explained (available from www.publicappointments.gov.uk/publications)

Charter Mark Standard (available from www.cabinetoffice.gov.uk/ chartermark/criteria.aspx)

Charity Commission

Charity Commission Publications (CC1), November 2007

The Charities Act 2006: What Trustees Need to Know, May 2007

The Essential Trustee: What You Need to Know (CC3), February 2007

Finding New Trustees: What Charities Need to Know (CC30), February 2007

The Hallmarks of an Effective Charity (CC60), April 2004

Registering as a Charity (CC21), October 2007

These and other useful publications are available from the Commission's website www.charity-commission.gov.uk.

Companies House

Company Formation (GBF1), August 2007

Directors and Secretaries Guide (GBA1), August 2007

Available from www.companieshouse.gov.uk

Many other useful publications are listed on the Companies House website.

Equality and Human Rights Commission

Code of Practice on Equal Pay, 1997

Code of Practice: Sex Discrimination

These and other publications relating to disability, race, gender and sexual orientation are available from www.equalityhumanrights.com

The Gambling Commission

Lotteries and the Law (Gambling Act 2005), 2007

Available from www.gamblingcommission.gov.uk

Health and Safety Commission

An Introduction to Health and Safety (INDG259REV1), 2003, free, ISBN 0717626857

Charity and Voluntary Workers – a Guide to Health and Safety at Work (HSG192), 2006, £13.50, ISBN 0717661857

Details of these and other useful publications are listed on the website www.hsebooks.co.uk

HM Revenue and Customs

Help sheets

Giving to Charity by Individuals

Giving to Charity by Businesses

Giving Land, Buildings, Shares and Securities to Charity

Fundraising Events: Exemption for Charities and Other Qualifying Bodies

Payroll Giving

Customer guides

These cover the most common areas of concern for charities and donors, including:

- Donations to charity
- Becoming a charity
- The tax advantages of being a charity
- Gift aid
- Trading and business activities

Help sheets and customer guides are available from www.hmrc.gov.uk/charities

VAT publications

Should I be Registered for VAT? (700/1), May 2002

The VAT Guide for Charities (701/1), May 2004

Clubs and Associations (701/5)

Available from www.hmrc.gov.uk (select 'VAT' from 'businesses and corporations')

Institute of Fundraising

Codes of Fundraising Practice

Available from www.institute-of-fundraising.org.uk/bestpractice

National Council for Voluntary Organisations

Good Governance – The Chair's Role, Dorothy Dalton, 2006, £10.00, ISBN 0 7199 1681 X

Good Governance – The Chief Executive's Role, Dorothy Dalton, 2007, £10.00, ISBN 978 0 7199 1682 3

The Good Trustee Guide (4th edn), Peter Dyer, 2003, £25, ISBN 0 7199 1610 0

VAT for Voluntary Organisations: A Step by Step Guide (6th edn), Graham Elliott, 2005, £10.00, ISBN 0 7199 1586 6

Office of the Scottish Charity Regulator (OSCR)

Guidance for Charity Trustees, 2006

Guidance for English and Welsh Charities, 2006 (for charities that want to register with OSCR)

Scottish Charity Accounting, 2007

These publications and other guidance for charities operating in Scotland can be downloaded from www.oscr.org.uk

The Scottish Executive

The McFadden Report, ISBN 1 4268 499 X

Available from www.scotland.gov.uk/publications

The Response of The Scottish Executive

Available from www.scotland.gov.uk/library5/justice/mcfadden_response.pdf

Stationery Office

Charities Act 1993 Ch 10, £11.30, ISBN 0105 432024

Charities Act 2006, Ch 50, £26.00, ISBN 0105 450065

Recreational Charities Act 1958 Ch 17 UK, £5.50, ISBN 0108 502252

www.opsi.gov.uk

Other publications

Butterworths Charity Law Handbook (2nd edn), Michael Scott and Simon Wethered, 2007, £99, ISBN/ISSN: 0405 708951 (www.lexisnexis.co.uk)

Charities Law and Practice (3rd edn), Elizabeth Cairns, Sweet & Maxwell, 1996, £130.00, ISBN 0421561908 (www.sweetandmaxwell.co.uk)

Develop Your Social Enterprise Idea, Office of the Third Sector/Business Link, 2007 (available from www.businesslink.gov.uk)

Handbook of Industrial and Provident Society Law (loose-leaf) I Snaith, Holyoake Books, 2001, £215.00 ISBN 0851952038 (available from www.co-op.ac.uk/store.asp)

Housing Association Law and Practice (4th edn), Professor John Alder & Dr Christopher Handy, Sweet & Maxwell, 2002, £134.00 ISBN 0421763906 (www.sweetmaxwell.co.uk)

Law and Practice Relating to Charities (3rd edn), Hubert Picarda, Butterworth, 1999, £289, ISBN 0406 921 475 (available from www.butterworths.co.uk)

Law of Trusts and Trustees (17th edn), Hon Justice Hayton with Professor Paul Matthews and Professor Charles Mitchell, Butterworth, 2006, £340, ISBN 1 405 708630 (available from www.butterworths.co.uk)

Management of Voluntary Organisations, Croner Publications, first year's subscription (including updates) £395.00 + VAI (available from www.croner.co.uk)

SCVO Guide to Constitutions and Charitable Status, Scottish Council of Voluntary Organisations, 2006, £35, ISBN 0954693000 (available from www.scvo.org.uk)

Tolley's Charities Manual (loose-leaf), Tolley, 1990, ISBN/ISSN 0751 508069 (available from www.lexisnexis.co.uk) £195.00 + updates

Tolley's Guide to the Charities Act 2006, Jean Paul da Costa, Thomas Eggar and Helen Harvie, Tolley, 2006, £64.95, ISBN 0754 527466 (available from www.lexisnexis.co.uk)

Tudor on Charities (9th edn) Jean Warburton, Debra Morris and NF Riddle, Sweet & Maxwell, 2003, £335, ISBN 0421 774 506 (available from www.sweetandmaxwell.co.uk)

Index